D0217650

Critical Guides to Spanish Texts

EDITED BY ALAN DEYERMOND & STEPHEN HART

ISABEL ALLENDE

La casa de los espíritus

Lloyd Davies

Lecturer in Spanish
University of Wales, Swansea

London
Grant & Cutler Ltd
2000

ISBN 0 7293 0419 1

DEPÓSITO LEGAL: V. 1.165 - 2000

Printed in Spain by
Artes Gráficas Soler, S.L., Valencia
for
GRANT & CUTLER LTD
55–57 GREAT MARLBOROUGH STREET, LONDON W1V 2AY

Contents

Preface

The edition of *La casa de los espíritus* referred to in this study is the 7th (Barcelona: Plaza & Janés, 1992). The abbreviated title, *La casa*, is used and page references are indicated thus: (100). Other novels by Allende cited in the text are as follows:

De amor y de sombra (Barcelona: Plaza & Janés: 1994).
Eva Luna (Barcelona: Plaza & Janés, 1992).
El plan infinito (Barcelona: Plaza & Janés, 1996).

In addition there are references to the following works by Gabriel García Márquez:

Cien años de soledad, ed. by Jacques Joset, Letras Hispánicas, 6th edn (Madrid: Cátedra, 1995). The abbreviated title, *Cien años*, is used.
'El ahogado más hermoso del mundo', in *La increíble y triste historia de la cándida Eréndira y de su abuela desalmada* (Madrid: Mondadori, 1987), pp. 43–51.
El otoño del patriarca (Madrid: Mondadori, 1987).

Works listed in the Bibliographical Note are referred to by an italic number, followed as required by a page-reference, e.g. (*4*, pp. 29–30).

I am indebted to the University of Wales Swansea for granting me a Sabbatical term in order to complete this study. My thanks are also due to the late Professor J. E. Varey, for his helpful comments on my original typescript, to Dr Stephen Hart, for subsequent advice, and to my colleagues at University of Wales Swansea, in particular to Professor Valerie Minogue, for her numerous suggestions, and to Mr J. B. Hall for his help and interest. Dr Luis Valenzuela advised me on specific historical points.

Sketty, Swansea
1998

1. Introduction

Isabel Allende was conceived on the high seas; her father, Tomás, a cousin of the future President, had been appointed Secretary of the Chilean embassy in Lima, where Isabel was born in 1942. Isabel's parents had three children despite being married for only four years. Just before the birth of the third, Tomás abandoned the family in the wake of a sex scandal which shook Lima's diplomatic community. Isabel's mother returned with her children to Santiago; there she met a divorcee, known to Isabel as Tío Ramón, and moved with him to Bolivia where he was to take up a diplomatic post. Isabel was then eleven years old and attended school in La Paz; it was a time of passionate writing, of 'páginas ardientes escritas en mis cuadernos' (*1*, p. 72). Tío Ramón was subsequently posted to Beirut where the family lived for three years. When Isabel was fifteen they returned to Chile; there she completed her secondary education and subsequently obtained a secretarial post with the United Nations Food and Agriculture Organization despite her bizarre behaviour at the interview — which clearly anticipates her future vocation. Asked to produce a typewritten letter, she wrote a 'carta de amor y despecho salpicada de faltas porque las teclas parecían tener vida propia [...]' (*1*, p. 111). This post gave her the opportunity to do television documentary work; she also contributed to Chile's first feminist publication, *Paula,* causing a scandal by publishing an interview with a self-confessed female adulterer who kept an apartment to facilitate romantic encounters. Isabel's marriage, in 1962, to her first husband Miguel Frías, an engineer, produced two children, Paula and Nicolás. In 1974, the year following the military coup in Chile, she took up residence in Venezuela where she combined journalistic work — a light-hearted column for the newspaper *El Nacional* — with school-teaching. It was only after the publication of *La casa de los espíritus*, in 1982, that she was able to

devote herself to full-time writing. This first novel was an immediate
success and its translation into English in 1985 gave Allende an
international reputation.

Her second novel, *De amor y de sombra*, followed in 1984,
and her third, *Eva Luna*, in 1987, the year of her divorce. In 1988 she
married an American lawyer, William Gordon, and subsequently
moved to California where she still lives. In 1989, she published
Cuentos de Eva Luna, a collection of twenty-three short stories. Her
fourth novel, *El plan infinito*, appeared in 1991. The following year
her daughter Paula died, at the age of twenty-eight, of porphyria, a
genetic disorder inherited from her father. This tragic episode
inspired Allende to write *Paula* (1994) which relates her daughter's
illness and death: the central focus is maternal anguish and emotional
trauma, but the work also provides useful insights into the writer's
strong family relationships, her spiritual resources, her social
commitment, her feminism, and her ideas about writing. A recent
latest publication, *Afrodita: cuentos, recetas y otros afrodisiacos*
(1997), complements *Paula* by offering a life-affirming celebration
of eroticism.

Allende's interest in politics emerges in a little-known
theatrical work, *El embajador* (1974), about the kidnapping of a
diplomat (*1*, p. 192). As the the niece of Salvador Allende, her
political commitment is hardly surprising; but although intimately
concerned with the fate of the Unidad Popular government, she
demonstrates in *Paula* an ability to distance herself from it. She
creates an impression of impartial observation rather than committed
support (she also had family ties, through her father-in-law, with the
political opposition): 'El sabotaje de la derecha y los errores de la
Unidad Popular, produjeron una crisis de proporciones nunca vistas
[...]' (*1*, p. 188). Such a balanced perspective does not, of course,
diminish her socialist credentials, but it does indicate freedom from
unreflecting political prejudice. As she told John Rodden in 1991:
'my writing is affected by politics. But I have never thought I could
write a novel to promote an ideological cause [...]' (*6*, p. 115). Her
fundamental liberalism is demonstrated in her personal life: despite
her political objections to the United States on account of its role in

the downfall of the Unidad Popular government, she took up residence there in order to 'entender su complejidad, conocerlo y aprender a amarlo' (*1*, p. 33). This open-mindedness and spirit of forgiveness is important for understanding her work, particularly *La casa de los espíritus*, whose ending on a note of reconciliation rather than revenge has been seen as a major weakness by some critics, as we shall see.

Until recently the name 'Allende' evoked a single, powerful image relating to the recent history of Chile: the figure of the world's first democratically elected Marxist president who came to power in 1970 and was brutally deposed in 1973. The name 'Allende' was firmly rooted then in the sphere of political history; but by the second half of the 1980s the political significance of this name was being supplemented by its reverberations within the world of literature.

Just as Allende the President aroused strong feelings on both sides of the political divide so did Isabel. Adored by her admirers — largely for her undisputed story-telling skills which combine imaginative 'magical realist' elements and emotive documentation of recent Chilean history — she was dismissed by her detractors as a popular rather than serious writer and a mere imitator of the supreme exponent of magical realism, Gabriel García Márquez.

Perhaps the most salient feature of Isabel Allende's writing is its accessibility: *La casa de los espíritus*, for example, can be appreciated by the ordinary reader. It does not demand the high level of literary competence required by much recent Latin American writing. The world of Allende's texts appears to reflect — unproblematically — the real Latin American world of cultural diversity, political strife, social inequality, patriarchal power, and incipient feminist rebellion. There is little overt interest in difficult issues, such as philosophy, literary theory, or technical artistry — the hallmarks of serious fiction as represented, for example, by the Boom generation of writers like Carlos Fuentes and Mario Vargas Llosa whose work came to prominence in the 1960s and 1970s. Allende has more in common with the post-Boom generation who turned away from their predecessors' encyclopaedic range of reference and technical virtuosity, though without turning back to the unproblematic, realist mode of writing dominant prior to 1940, when the innovative currents of the Latin American *Nueva novela* began to gather strength. Post-Boom writers, by comparison with the Boom, are generally more accessible and dismissive of the traditional division between high and low art, often incorporating elements of popular culture (usually ironized) in their work. The post-Boom embraces several distinct styles of writing, ranging through testimonial literature from autobiography to oral history represented by Elena Poniatowska (Mexico, 1932–), political documentary committed to conventional narrative and observed reality, represented by Antonio Skármeta (Chile, 1940–) and the postmodernist, citational text associated with Manuel Puig (Argentina, 1934–1990). Elements of all three strands can be found in *La casa de los espíritus* which, on the one hand, provides a testimonial view of personal suffering and a forthright political message while, on the other, it offers shifting narrative perspectives and stylistic heterogeneity.[1]

It is tempting to use such terms as 'postmodernism' when discussing *La casa de los espíritus* but critics should be cautious when applying Western critical concepts to Latin American writing: Santiago Colás warns against unfocused assimilations which exclude the 'specific social and political conditions out of which that [Latin American] culture has emerged' and George Yúdice similarly stresses that postmodern theories need to be 'deconstructed and reconstructed' in relation to Latin American contexts' (*27*, p. xi; *34*, p. 9). Shaw's reservations focus on the usual context of debate

---

[1] For further information on the post-Boom see Donald L. Shaw, 'Towards a Description of the Post-Boom', *Bulletin of Hispanic Studies*, 66 (1989), 87–94. Some close affinities between Skármeta and Allende can be inferred from Shaw's view of Skármeta as equally committed to 'la aventura de la palabra' on the one hand and to conventional narrative and 'observed reality' on the other. Donald Shaw, *Antonio Skármeta and the Post Boom* (Hanover, NH: Ediciones del Norte, 1994), pp. 16–17. Elsewhere Shaw analyses Allende's ambivalent view of reality which she often treats as ultimately unknowable but also explores as though it were capable of decipherment (*22*, pp. 53–72).

about postmodernism — sociopolitical rather than specifically literary (22, p. 168). These strictures are not without point, though it is well to bear in mind that it was an Argentine writer, Jorge Luis Borges, who played a pivotal role in shaping the international corpus of postmodernist writing, which has since been enriched by other Latin American writers such as Julio Cortázar, Carlos Fuentes, and Manuel Puig. Overuse has deprived such terms as 'postmodernism', 'feminism', and 'magical realism' of much of their original force, but they remain useful for analysing *La casa de los espíritus*.

'Postmodernism' retains a central core of significance relating to the problematic nature of language and representation (thus the proliferation in Borges's work of images of mirrors, copies, duplications) and the dislocation of binary concepts (good/bad, truth/falsehood, reason/nonsense) and fixed sexual identity. Postmodernist writers tend to problematize language as a reliable instrument of communication by highlighting linguistic texture and slippage, through techniques such as punning and etymological word play. Postmodernism challenges the concept of any monological or univalent structure of signification, postulating rather the destabilization of meaning and knowledge. One important current within postmodernism is feminism which, through its powerful two-edged discourse, offers a radical critique of the master narratives of modern man. On the political front it challenges the order of patriarchal society, while on the epistemological, it questions the structure of representation.[2] It is therefore the most potent of the repressed or marginalized discourses. The negative side of postmodernism, from a Latin American perspective, is its capacity to co-opt the margins and to subsume differences — sexual, political,

---

[2] For a clear exposition of feminism in relation to postmodernism, see Craig Owens, 'The Discourse of the Others: Feminists and Post-modernism', in *The Anti-Aesthetic: Essays on Postmodern Culture* (Seattle, WA: Bay Press, 1983), pp. 57–77.

racial, cultural — in a 'new, sophisticated economy of "sameness"'
— thereby neutralizing the 'other'.[3]

Within the broad sociopolitical focus of Allende's works, gender issues assume particular importance, though her treatment seems untouched by the extensive academic theorizing on the subject produced in Latin America as well as in Europe and the United States. Allende's condemnation of patriarchy may appear blunt and unsophisticated, deriving as it does from lived experience rather than from textbook formulations. Her own family circumstances inevitably predisposed her in favour of female solidarity and independence from the remote male figure: her relationship with her mother began in the womb when her mother 'estableció con ella un diálogo permanente que no ha cesado hasta hoy' (*1*, p. 120). Though she cannot remember 'ese período intrauterino', it is clearly significant, pointing to Allende's prioritizing of the body over the intellect, and intuition over reason; it may also remind the reader of Julia Kristeva's concept of the 'semiotic', a stage of pre-verbal consciousness which, in the case of the infant, determines its bodily orientation towards the mother. The (female) body is fundamentally important in Allende's writing, both literally, in terms of its physical functions and cycles, and metaphorically as conditioning the sensuous, fluid texture of her language and style.[4] The father — a figure unknown to the young Isabel — represents absence and lack (so reversing, in a sense, the psychoanalytic stereotyping of woman), and within the family is treated as a taboo subject: 'papá es una palabra prohibida' (*1*, p. 46). The male principle is primarily associated with authority and Allende's sensitivity to various kinds of authority is indicated by her frequent use of the term 'patriarchal':

---

[3] Nelly Richard comments perceptively on this aspect of postmodernism. See 'Postmodernism and Periphery', in *Postmodernism: A Reader*, ed. by Thomas Docherty (Hemel Hempstead: Harvester Wheatsheaf, 1993), pp. 463–70 (p. 468).

[4] While Allende is aware of the main currents in feminist criticism she is not significantly influenced by them. She frequently protests that her work does not offer the poetic depth which students seek in it and urges her readers to enjoy her texts 'en vez de analizar y hacer similitudes y buscar influencias [...]' (*4*, p. 58).

the benign influence of the mother figure is balanced by 'poderosas figuras patriarcales' — such as her grandfather — who stirred her rebellious instincts against male authority (*4*, p. 52). If this authority blighted her familiar private space, its effect on the public national space was to be devastating. In 'Writing as an Act of Hope', Allende refers to male domination through the patriarchal regime (*2*, p. 54). In contrast with the mother figure who, through childbirth, 'encarna el poder femenino en el universo', (*1*, pp. 22–23), male authority, capable of erupting with murderous violence as it did during the 1973 military coup, represents for Allende a negative, anti-life force. Authority is multifaceted, inhabiting both private and public spheres, and can even contaminate the space of writing in the guise of what Allende calls a 'paternalistic attitude' (*2*, p. 59).

Personal experience conditions many aspects of Allende's writing, particularly those which might appear fanciful and furthest removed from the real world. The catalyst for the writing of *La casa* was her grandfather's decision to die once he had read the entire *Encyclopaedia Britannica*, learned by heart the *Diccionario de la Real Academia*, and finally lost interest in *telenovelas*. Isabel decides to write him a letter but her writing becomes a constant nocturnal activity guided by the spirit of her late grandmother: 'escribía sin esfuerzo alguno, sin pensar, porque mi abuela clarividente me dictaba' (*1*, pp. 303–04). This writing surpassed its original purpose and migrated from the epistolary to the novelistic genre. Such crossing of boundaries underlies much of Allende's writing: for her the real is not necessarily the visible, the reasonable and the logical; rather, such non-rational elements as intuition, dream, clairvoyance, and communication with the dead inhabit her everyday world. Her practice of talking to spirits might appear strange but to her constitutes normal behaviour — suggesting that she is more in tune with the values of indigenous America than with those of rational Europe where the spiritual life has been devalued. While her daughter lay dying, Isabel maintained a mystical contact with her: 'yo me comunicaba con ella en sueños' (*4*, p. 54). When the contact was lost Isabel resorted to magicians, psychics and homeopathy. Another broken frontier allows 'real' and 'fictional' characters to intermingle: one of Allende's uncles used to tell her that fictional characters leave the pages to wander around the house at night (*1*, p. 40). In *La casa de los espíritus* the reverse process takes place as real people enter the fictional world: Salvador Allende, the dictator Augusto Pinochet, and the poet Pablo Neruda.[5]

Isabel Allende's ideas on writing are devoid of intellectual pretensions. She has little knowledge of critical practice — 'tampoco había leído crítica y no sospechaba que los libros se analizan en universidades con la misma seriedad con que se estudian los astros en el firmamento' (*1*, p. 306; *2*, p. 44) — and is taken aback by critics finding unintended symbolism in her work. She claims to write in a kind of trance which accords with her view of literature as a 'manera mágica de atrapar a alguien por el cuello y decirle: mira, así estamos, esto es lo que existe [...]' (*4*, p. 56). Such apparent naiveté combined with habitual self-deprecation — 'Yo soy una cuentacuentos'; 'Me siento como un pirata que se hubiera lanzado al abordaje de las letras' (*12*, p. 99; *21*, p. 21) has served to reinforce the prejudices of critics instinctively hostile towards her work because of its popular qualities, its allegedly emotional rather than intellectual appeal and its traditional (and, supposedly, unchallenging) narrative form that facilitates easy consumption.[6] For several critics, too, Allende's literary status is hopelessly undermined by her overdependence on techniques largely pioneered by García Márquez. Her rather effortless assumption of best-seller status has inevitably caused further resentment, intensified, no doubt, by the extravagant claims made on her behalf on the other side of the

---

[5] In its use of historical characters as literary protagonists *La casa* makes contact with the New Historical novel, identified by Seymour Menton as the dominant trend in contemporary Latin American fiction (*31*, p. 14). See below pp. 97–98.

[6] While Shaw sees *La casa* as exemplifying the Post-Boom's 'need to escape from [...] the constricting intellectualism of the Boom' (*22*, p. 72), he remains puzzled by the apparent lack of intellectual cohesion in *La casa* where a disturbing sense of determinism confronts a positive vision of future progress: 'It is not clear how these different notions fit together' (*22*, p. 71). For further discussion, see below, pp. 98–103.

critical divide.[7] But there is a complexity about Allende which largely awaits proper investigation: the magical realist elements which often hover undecidedly between positive and negative evaluations; the peculiarly feminist impulse and the nature of the relationship between women, maternity, and writing; the metafictional aspects focusing on the process of textual production; and the deployment of various discourses which divert attention from story to language. One of my purposes in the following chapters will be to investigate the balance of disparate and often contradictory forces which govern her writing and thereby to argue for a new perception of Allende's complexity which might complement her appeal as a popular writer.

Although critical reception of *La casa de los espíritus* and subsequent works has been generally favourable, there remain serious doubts about Allende's literary credentials which have led to her exclusion from the canon of modern Latin American authors: the Chilean critic, Cedomil Goic, excludes her from his monumental *Historia y crítica de la literatura hispanoamericana* (1988) and there are several other less striking omissions.[8] Some critics, however, include Allende's work within a progressive tradition of Latin

---

[7] The blurb carried by the early editions of *La casa de los espíritus* claimed that Allende completed the Boom, which previously lacked female representation: 'Faltaba entre ellos, por lo menos, *una* novelista. La impecable desenvoltura estilística, la lucidez histórica y social y la coherencia estética de *La casa de los espíritus* hacen que Isabel Allende acceda de golpe a dicha cúspide con su primera novela.'

[8] Full reference is *Historia y crítica de la literatura hispanoamericana*, 3 vols (Barcelona: Crítica, 1988–1991), vol.3. Debra A. Castillo makes two passing references to Allende in *Talking Back: Toward a Latin American Feminist Literary Criticism* (Ithaca: Cornell University Press, 1992), pp. 23, 31. The first reference may explain why Allende's work is ignored: it makes the dubious claim that she 'arrived on the "Boom" scene twenty years after its vogue but with the same assumptions intact' (p. 23). The crucial differences between *La casa de los espíritus* and García Márquez's *Cien años de soledad*, demonstrate that Allende and her feminist mode of writing cannot be assimilated by the (male) Boom generation whose masterful voices and totalizing vision underpin a patriarchal artistry that goes against the grain of Allende's most basic instincts.

American women's writing (*34*, p. 75) and my aim here is to reinforce this perception of her as a serious feminist writer.[9]

---

[9] In *A Literature of Their Own: British Women Novelists from Brontë to Lessing*, new rev. edn. (London: Virago, 1982), p. 13, Elaine Showalter applies the terms 'feminine', 'feminist' and 'female' to the three major phases she identifies in the historical development of women: 'feminine' relates to the imitation of the historical tradition and internationalization of its standards of art; 'feminist' corresponds to protest against these standards; 'female' refers to self-discovery and search for identity. While I do not follow Showalter's negative inflection of the term 'feminine', my use of 'feminist' and 'female' corresponds broadly with hers.

2. *Contexts:*

The historical background

La casa de los espíritus traces the triumphs and adversities of four women: Nívea, Clara, Blanca, and Alba. Allende's positive portrayal of her women is indicated explicitly by their names which represent variations on the theme of whiteness. The novel opens in the early part of this century, shortly before Clara, then aged ten, stopped speaking (76). (She subsequently broke her nine years' silence in order to announce her intention of marrying Esteban who had returned to the capital following the presidential elections of 1920.) The action is being recalled in 1973 by the narrator, Alba, whose account, based on her grandmother Clara's notebooks, is written fifty years after Clara recorded the important events of her life — a task she had begun at the age of ten (11, 15). At the novel's conclusion with the military coup of 1973, one of the surviving women, Alba's mother, Blanca, is living in exile in Canada while the other, Alba herself, continues to live in the shadow of state terror in Chile. Clara's husband, Esteban Trueba, is in some ways the lynchpin character, being both a major player throughout the action and a forceful contributor to the writing of the narrative. However, the main narrator is Alba who begins by acknowledging her dependence on Clara's notebooks — 'Barrabás llegó a la familia por vía marítima, anotó la niña Clara con su delicada caligrafía' (9) — and makes repeated reference to them throughout the narrative.

Edwin Williamson describes *La casa de los espíritus* as a magical realist novel that 'traced the history of twentieth-century Chile through four generations of women, culminating in the protagonists' incarceration after the military coup of 1973' (*45*, p. 562). Writing here as a historian, Williamson recognizes the sociopolitical backbone of a work whose title might suggest the

predominance of otherworldly concerns. But of course Isabel
Allende is the niece of the Marxist president whose pursuit of social
justice, so long denied to the majority of his fellow Chileans, was
brutally thwarted by military intervention in September 1973, and
her novel is, in a sense, a testament to Salvador Allende's enduring
efforts to bring about change (he stood for president three times
before his election in 1970). The novel is written in the magical
realist mode which can be interpreted as an artistic response both to
the grander scale of Latin American geography and to the continent's
stark sociopolitical realities — as seen from a European or
Europeanized perspective. The Uruguayan writer, Eduardo Galeano,
points out that 'el abismo que en América Latina se abre entre el
bienestar de pocos y la desgracia de muchos es infinitamente mayor
que en Europa o en Estados Unidos' (*41*, p. 446). Yet the northern
part of Chile is rich in copper and nitrates (Chile's victory over Peru
and Bolivia in the War of the Pacific, 1879–83, increased her mineral
wealth) and, by the end of the nineteenth century, export of minerals
to Europe had become the mainstay of the economy. Such natural
resources could have provided a high standard of living for all
sectors of the population but it accrued in the main to the mine-
owners who, together with the *latifundistas* (holders of vast estates in
the countryside), formed an élite minority, comprising approximately
10% of the population, bent on preserving their status in the face of
social pressures coming from below. In *La casa de los espíritus*,
Esteban Trueba represents both groups since he begins his working
life as a mine-owner before returning to the family estate — *Las Tres
Marías* — where he makes his fortune. He flaunts his affluence,
acquiring a second residence, a town house, known as 'la gran casa
de la esquina', which he has built in the foreign style. Bolstered by
his crude social Darwinism, Esteban remains indifferent to the
misfortunes of others. He berates and beats Pedro Tercero García,
the son of his foreman, for distributing subversive literature on the
estate, and rails against 'politicastros del demonio' (164) who
include the new Socialist candidate, Salvador Allende. Social
violence becomes widespread and the story of the socialist worker,
murdered by the land-owning Sánchez brothers and hanged from a

telegraph pole, is recalled by Blanca (Esteban's daughter) as a warning to her lover, Pedro Tercero (166). Clara, who opposes her husband's self-interested conservatism, instructs the women and children of the estate in matters of hygiene and education and her son, Jaime, a doctor, gives almost all that he has to the poor. But the divisions resulting from social class run particularly deep in Chilean society and are almost impossible to overcome, as the fraught liaison between Blanca and Pedro Tercero indicates.

The great estates had remained unchanged for 300 years and the largely *mestizo* peasantry was compliant — unlike the mine-workers of the nitrate deserts of the north who introduced working-class militancy to Chile at the end of the nineteenth century. But although the urban mineworkers did not share the traditionally deferential attitude of the peasants there was little legal opportunity to improve their situation since voting rights were restricted: the exclusion of women and illiterate men until the 1950s reduced potential voters to 20% of the population. In *La casa*, Clara's mother, Nívea, remarkable for her progressive and independent social ideas, involves herself in the struggle for female suffrage, even visiting factories in an attempt to rally working-class women to the cause. As late as 1920 only 5% of the population voted and it was not until 1949 that voting rights were extended to women. The landowners, in any case, controlled the parliamentary system, assuring the Conservative and Liberal parties enough congressional power to curb any radical presidential proposals. In *La casa* landowners like Esteban bribe the peasants, inducing them to vote for the status quo: 'mira que los liberales y los radicales son todos unos pendejos y los comunistas son unos ateos, hijos de puta, que se comen a los niños' (73). In urban areas, however, strike action became a much-used weapon: between 1890 and 1910 two hundred and fifty strikes took place. After 1919 anarchist influence declined following the failure of a general strike called in Santiago, and socialism and communism increased their influence. The Chilean Communist Party, founded in 1922, was to become the most powerful in Latin America.

The 1891 civil war was fought largely over the issue of presidential authority (the loser, President Balmaceda, had been locked in stalemate with Congress whose support he had lost), and subsequently power was transferred from the executive to the Congress. In *La casa* Allende refers to the 1918 parliamentary elections in which Severo del Valle, the father of one of the central figures of the novel, Clara, is set to participate as the Liberal Party candidate for a Southern province that he had never visited. He withdraws when his daughter Rosa dies after drinking poisoned brandy intended for him. This episode suggests that women are often the major victims of political conflict conducted by men. The autopsy, performed by Dr Cuevas and his assistant, who dismember the body, serves as an ominous portent of the violation of the body politic which will come later. Severo's side accuses the oligarchy of the crime and claims that the Conservatives — later to be represented in the Senate by Severo's son-in-law, Esteban (215) — were unable to forgive one of their own class for deserting to the Liberals (37–38). By this time, however, differences between the Conservative and Liberal Parties — both of which represented the great landowners of the Central Valley and supplied the nation's presidents and congressmen — were slight, and Severo's opportunistic affiliation to the Liberals may have had more to do with his atheism and freemasonry (11) than with practical politics.

In the 1920 presidential elections, Arturo Alessandri, the Liberal Alliance candidate, came to power, supported by sections of the oligarchy eager to placate the masses with minimal social change. Esteban's celebration of the election results should be seen in this light. Alessandri's proposals for social and constitutional change were thwarted by the resolute opposition of congress (*45*, p. 487) and Esteban's class interests were to remain unchallenged, at least for the time being. In 1924 the armed forces intervened to shore up the president, and the constitution of the following year — destined to remain in force until 1973 — was intended to strengthen the power of the executive. In 1925, following the strong-arm tactics employed by Carlos Ibáñez, the Minister of War, against an increasingly restive labour force, Alessandri resigned and Ibáñez himself assumed the presidency in 1927. Ominously he continued to blame the country's political corruption and class conflict on the parliamentary system which was undoubtedly weak and flawed but had served to foster democratic principles and political tolerance. Countering this liberal tradition was a militaristic creed widely diffused by a compulsory military service law of 1900 which enabled thousands of Chileans to see patriotism and history from the military perspective. But although Ibáñez curtailed certain freedoms such as that of the press, he channelled resources towards public works and education; it is arguable that the Ibáñez era brought the Chilean population as a whole a higher standard of living than ever before.

The military, always a force to be reckoned with in Chilean politics, was alarmed by the rising number of strikes which were not entirely confined to urban areas: the first recorded rural strike had taken place in 1911. Ibáñez's Labour Code of 1931 restricted union activity and institutionalized the practice of state intervention in industrial relations. However, the effects of the Wall Street crash of 1929 were felt keenly in Chile and plunged the government into unpopularity. Ibáñez resigned in July 1931; his tenure of office had been comparatively short but through his rejection of liberal democracy and determined quest to recast the political and social life of the country according to authoritarian principles, he had established a precedent for the brutal military operation of the 1970s. Following Ibáñez's resignation, several short-term régimes governed the country (including a 'Socialist Republic' which lasted for 100 days). The presidential elections of 1932 restored civilian government and from then until 1973, somewhat against the odds in view of social conflict and natural disaster, Chile emerged as the only Latin American country to enjoy a stable democracy free from military intervention. This period is somewhat reminiscent of the early Republican era (1830–70) when the country enjoyed virtually unbroken constitutional stability and a system of political pluralism which gave her the reputation of being the England of South America.

By 1890, 70% of the Chilean nitrate industry was controlled by the British. The economic effect of World War I, however, was to

transfer influence from Britain to the United States, and American
investors acquired nitrate and mining properties, especially copper
and iron. By the end of the war the Americans controlled over 87%
of Chilean copper production; by 1930, U.S. investment accounted
for 70% of foreign investment in Chile. Subsequently, the rise of
economic nationalism and state-led development, embodied in the
Corporación de Fomento (CORFO), established in 1939, exposed the
contradictions between the national interest and the interests of U.S.
foreign policies or companies: the Right as well as the Left resented
the involvement in Chile of American copper firms who repatriated
their profits; but it was not until 1970 that the foreign stranglehold on
the nation's resources was seriously challenged. As Eduardo Galeano
notes: 'Hasta la victoria electoral de las fuerzas de la Unidad Popular
en 1970, los mayores yacimientos del metal rojo continuaban en
manos de la Anaconda Copper Mining Co. y la Kennecott Copper
Co. [...] En medio siglo, ambas habían remitido cuatro mil millones
de dólares desde Chile a sus casas matrices [...]' (*41*, p. 234). In his
Canto general the great Chilean poet, Pablo Neruda, uses the image
of the all-consuming serpent to highlight the exploitation of Chilean
workers by the Anaconda Copper Mining Co.:

> la gran serpiente se los come,
> los disminuye, los tritura,
> los cubre de baba maligna,
> los arroja por los caminos,
> los mata con la policía,
> los hace pudrir en Pisagua,
> los encarcela, los escupe,
> compra un Presidente traidor
> que los insulta y los persigue,
> los mata de hambre en las llanuras
> de la inmensidad arenosa. (from *Canto
> general*, Part v)

Chile did not break off relations with the Axis powers until
January 1943 and proved thereafter to be a somewhat reluctant

supporter of the Allied cause (*40*, p. 298). After 1945, the logic of the Cold War was used to justify intensified U.S. involvement in a country seen as an important battlegound between Communism and the Free World. The 1946 election, mentioned in *La casa* (175), was won with Communist support by Gabriel González Videla of the Radical Party which represented mainly middle-class interests. (It is at a local Conservative dinner in 1946 that Esteban meets the effeminate and affluent Count Jean de Satigny whom he will later manipulate into marrying Blanca, then pregnant by Pedro Tercero.) President González Videla quickly turned against his old allies, however, and undertook a vigorous anti-Communist drive, even establishing a concentration camp for left-wing militants in an abandoned mine in the northern desert. In 1948 the Law for the Permanent Defence of Democracy outlawed the Communist Party. As Williamson notes, it was at this time that Neruda began to compose his *Canto general* which 'expressed a vision of Latin America's historical destiny in which socialist revolution was identified with genuine national independence from foreign imperialists and indigenous traitors' (*45*, p. 492). In the 1952 presidential elections Carlos Ibáñez, promising an end to corruption and defence of economic sovereignty, returned to power supported by a variety of parties including a newly organized Feminist Party. His electoral reform of 1958 drastically curtailed the power of the landlords in Chilean politics through increased penalties for electoral fraud and bribery; but his economic policies were a resounding failure. With the advent of the secret ballot, landowners could no longer control the votes of their workers; compulsory voting increased the pressure and ensured the demise of the hacienda system. In the 1958 presidential elections, mentioned in *La casa* (213), Salvador Allende, representing an alliance of Socialists and Communists known as the Frente de Acción Popular (FRAP), lost narrowly to Jorge Alessandri (son of the former president) who was supported by Liberals and Conservatives.

The closeness of the result is highlighted in *La casa*: 'ganaron las elecciones los mismos de siempre, pero por tan escaso margen que todo el país se alertó' (213). Not surprisingly, Esteban is alarmed by the rise of the Left and determines to stand for the forthcoming parliamentary elections. As Clara foresees, he is duly elected a Conservative senator. He enjoys a successful political career, being re-elected on several occasions (290–91). However, his paranoia about what he calls 'el cáncer marxista' (291) is eventually justified by events. The establishment of a socialist government in Cuba in 1959 was a landmark event with the potentiality to change the course of Latin American politics. The U.S. response was the Alliance for Progress which included commitment to agrarian reform. In the 1964 presidential elections Allende again lost narrowly, this time to the Christian Democrat, Eduardo Frei, who stood for radical reform through legal, peaceful means. Although the party was founded only in 1957, the roots of Christian Democracy go back at least to the beginning of the century, when Catholic clergy and politicians took an active part in social affairs including involvement in unionization (the papal encyclical *De rerum novarum* of 1891 encouraged social action by the clergy). In government the Christian Democrats attempted to carry out far-reaching changes including Chileanization of the copper industry and agrarian reform; Galeano acknowledges that Frei 'abrió el cauce a la reforma agraria radical' (*41*, p. 211), a task resumed later by the Socialists.

In 1964 rural unions hardly existed; by 1969 there were more than four hundred. The unions, however, adopted obstructionist tactics and supported land occupations and illegal strikes. Frei himself adopted measures which would increase rather than diminish Chile's economic dependence. In *La casa*, there is a graphic description of the turbulence of the months preceding the presidential elections of 1970. To the dismay of his son, Jaime, Esteban participates in a foreign-supported campaign to vilify the Communists, using 'afiches truculentos donde aparecía una madre barrigona y desolada, que intentaba inútilmente arrebatar su hijo a un soldado comunista que se lo llevaba a Moscú' (318). In the elections Allende was the candidate of Unidad Popular (FRAP having formed the backbone of a new coalition of six leftist parties), and, campaigning on the basis of a 'transition to socialism', gained a slim majority. His victory caused panic amongst his opponents whose misplaced confidence in another victory is highlighted by Esteban's prediction: 'Ganaremos los de siempre' (322). Allende's régime was characterized by intensified political turmoil and more blatant U.S. interference in Chilean internal affairs.

The U.P. programme included the establishment of a people's assembly; increased participation of workers and peasants at all levels of policymaking and extension of the public sector by expropriating all agricultural estates above eighty hectares: in *La casa*, Esteban's estate is expropriated (337). Almost as many farms were expropriated in the first year of the U.P. government as in the whole term of the previous régime. The large copper mines were nationalized and their assets transferred to the nation, but small private firms were allowed to continue operating. All aspects of life became politicized and politics became polarized; party loyalty was undermined by the rise of new movements known as *poder popular* which weakened the authority of government (*40*, p. 340).

Allende headed a precarious coalition divided over the type and pace of reform. As a Marxist, he inevitably drew bitter opposition both from within the country (which had a large and influential middle class by 1970) and from the United States which sought to foment unrest and encourage opposition. In *La casa* we read that people besieged the banks in a scramble to withdraw their savings; property values declined and the airlines could not cope with the mass exodus: 'en pocas horas el país se dividió en dos bandos irreconciliables y la división comenzó a extenderse entre todas las familias' (324). Esteban is incredulous in the face of defeat — although he himself had long warned of the likelihood of such an eventuality. Having proclaimed his own side the 'defensor de la democracia' (322), he now participates in a top-level conspiracy to overthrow the elected government by promoting economic destabilization (325). This campaign was to receive active United States support: while American economic aid was reduced or cut off, military assistance was increased. Later U.S. congressional hearings exposed the Nixon administration's disruptive tactics. To compound matters, Chile remained economically dependent on the U.S. which supplied nearly 40% of her imports and was her main international public creditor. Business confidence was damaged by the increasingly voluble demands from workers for expropriation of farms and factories and also by the uncertain future of private enterprise which led to the widespread selling of equipment and assets rather than to growth in investment.

By mid-1973, inflation had exceeded 300%, which reduced real income levels to below those of 1970. The Left became increasingly divided and the Right remained bent on disruption. In *La casa* we read that shops ran out of supplies as panic buying became widespread; the black market boomed (330). Both Blanca and Esteban take to hoarding — foodstuffs in the case of the daughter, arms in that of the father. Alba, however, raids both stores: the food is channelled to the poor while the arms fall into the hands of Esteban's sworn enemies via Alba's lover, Miguel. When *Las Tres Marías* is expropriated by the government, Esteban can only vent his anger by confronting its new owners, but he is taken hostage. A massive strike of shopkeepers and professional workers in October 1972 was precipitated by the independent truckers' association protesting against government plans to create a state-owned trucking enterprise. In *La casa* the political motives of the truckers are emphasized: 'a la segunda semana fue evidente que no era un asunto laboral, sino político, y que no pensaban volver al trabajo' (330). Women use pots and pans to demonstrate against the Allende regime and doctors go on strike (343–44). The government responded by declaring a partial state of emergency. Allende appointed the army commander-in-chief, Carlos Prats, to serve as Minister of the Interior, which he combined with his army post. Prats successfully negotiated with the truckers and the immediate crisis was overcome; but, significantly, the military had played the role of arbiter in the settlement of a major political conflict.

At the congressional elections of March 1973 the opposition fought as an alliance which included the Christian Democrats and the conservative Partido Nacional, with the aim of achieving a two-thirds majority which would permit Allende's impeachment. They failed and the results indicated that the U.P. coalition still enjoyed considerable popular support. However, between March and

September 1973 extremist militancy on both Left and Right intensified. The Christian Democrat-led strike at the El Teniente copper mine lasted two months and brought the government into direct conflict not with the *momios* (the U.P. term for supporters of the old order) but with organized labour. General Prats resigned after a demonstration by hundreds of wives of military officers outside his residence, and was replaced as chief of staff by General Augusto Pinochet, who entered Allende's cabinet as Minister of War, and was believed to be a democrat. On September 11 he carried out the coup which resulted in the death of Salvador Allende, following aerial bombardment of the presidential palace. This action inaugurated a long period of repressive government and state terror in which thousands of Chileans were to lose their lives. Chapter 13 of *La casa* covers the military coup and its aftermath: Jaime is summoned to the Presidential Palace, which is already in turmoil as the coup takes hold. The President makes his final broadcast to the nation. Jaime falls into the hands of the military but refuses to comply with their demand that he go on television to confirm their claim that a drunken president had committed suicide. Esteban's celebrations of the end of socialism coincide with Jaime's torture at the hands of the country's new rulers. Esteban is not invited to participate in the new government and its increasingly blatant authoritarianism and brutality force him to accept a report that his son had died. Writing in 1978 Galeano says that 'en Chile la cacería dejó un saldo de treinta mil muertos' (*41*, p. 467). The military's implementation of monetarist economic policies following the Friedman model can be reconciled with their political objectives: indiscriminate application of market principles destabilize social agencies and institutions and sought to promote the privatization of the social sector, thereby rendering collective action redundant. In *La casa* Isabel Allende indicates that the new economic order generated an affluent class of economists and investors at one extreme and a growing army of beggars at the other (361–62).

The responsibility of the United States for the collapse of the Allende regime was considerable, as Galeano emphasizes: 'desde 1970, Kissinger y los servicios de informaciones prepararon cuidadosamente la caída de Allende. Millones de dólares fueron distribuidos entre los enemigos del gobierno legal de la Unidad Popular' (*41*, pp. 448–49). Brian Loveman, on the other hand, claims that the real culprits were the ultra-leftists whose fanaticism and recklessness facilitated reaction rather than revolution (Miguel of *La casa* fits this category); there were important sections of Allende's own Socialist Party which supported the *vía insurreccional* rather than the *vía pacífica* (*44*, p. 307). The government itself was also partly responsible: it failed to come to terms with its natural ally, the Christian Democrats, rejecting the overtures of that party both before and after the 1970 election; it also continued to use the rhetoric of revolution which bore little relation to its practical policies but which nevertheless aroused fear and alarm in many ordinary people, helping thereby to create an atmosphere of uncertainty conducive to military intervention.

The brutality of the military regime is reflected in the closing episodes of the novel. When *Las Tres Marías* reverts to Esteban he exacts terrible revenge on the *inquilinos* who all disperse to other regions. While Blanca and Pedro Tercero go into exile in Canada, their daughter Alba remains in the country and harbours fugitives in the unused rooms of her grandfather's house. Her activities are soon detected and she is interrogated and tortured by her own blood relative, Esteban García (Esteban Trueba's illegitimate grandson). She is placed in the *perrera*, a small, dark, and airless cell which prisoners can endure for only short periods of time. Her eventual release results from the intercession of a prostitute, Tránsito Soto, acting on the request of Esteban who had done her a good turn years before, setting her up in business.

The Epilogue is written in the first person, by Alba, on the day after Esteban's death. She acknowledges that the idea of writing the story was Esteban's (409), and that he himself contributed several pages. On completing his writing he lay down to die in Clara's bed. Alba concludes her narrative on a renewed note of reconciliation and forgiveness — sentiments which Esteban himself had come to share. Her final reference is to Clara's notebooks, the basis of much of the narrative, and the text ends as it had begun — by quoting the first line of Clara's first notebook — 'Barrabás llegó a la familia por vía marítima'.

It is against this background of social injustice and tyranny, resistance, democratic breakthrough, and renewed repression that the plot of *La casa* develops. Clara's intuitive and clairvoyant powers and her progressive political instincts are contrasted with the self-seeking conservatism of her *machista* husband, Esteban. The text's most positive notes emerge in the development of female independence of action — Clara turns her back on Esteban while Blanca does not flinch in her role of unmarried mother — and of female political awareness as manifested in Nívea's interest in female emancipation, Clara's insight and practicality and Alba's self-sacrifice in the cause of democracy. Esteban Trueba is portrayed negatively as the representative of male aggression, directed on occasion against his own family, but he is partially redeemed at the end by his recognition of his past errors and by the turning away from his male violence towards female serenity and spirit of reconciliation. The novel highlights political corruption, social deprivation, and heroic female resistance to male tyranny at the level of both the individual family and national government.

Apart from its testimonial impact the text is notable for its literary attributes and preoccupations, its diversity of perspectives and styles, and its self-conscious references to its own creation, as we shall see.

The Literary Background: the Literary Father

'At last literary daughters can think back through literary mothers — whom they regard with "mingled feelings of rivalry and anxiety"'.[10] The Chilean writer Luisa María Bombal (1910–80) can certainly be seen as a kind of literary mother to Allende: she valued those mysterious aspects of life that she felt to be ignored or undermined by rational society: 'Hemos organizado una existencia lógica sobre

---

[10] Pam Morris, *Literature and Feminism* (Oxford: Basil Blackwell, 1993), pp. 70–71.

un pozo de misterios.'[11] Her female characters resemble Allende's: in them emotion and intuition are largely uninhibited by the dictates of rigour and logic, qualities often associated with the male psyche. For Bombal, woman is a natural being, her long hair representing her femininity and affinity with nature: she is associated with the earth and the sea (as are Allende's Rosa, Clara, and Alba). In *La última niebla* the mist introduces ambiguity, blurring the divide between the logical and visible (associated with the male) and the illogical, that is, the abstract and invisible (associated with the female); in general, though, Bombal's work remains focused on that enduring conflict between 'lo femenino enraigado en lo maravilloso ancestral y lo masculino racionalizador'. Her female characters are passive, conforming to the conventional roles they are expected to play and withdrawing into themselves (Guerra Cunningham, pp. 198, 39). In portraying women prepared to oppose their sexual and economic exploitation in a male society, Allende performs an 'act of creative correction' in relation to her predecessor's work.[12]

However, the literary father, in the form of García Márquez, casts a longer shadow than any female writer over Allende's work, symbolically extending to the literary sphere the patriarchal domination that operates in the social sphere. While acknowledging his influence, Allende unsurprisingly attempts to play it down: '*Cien años* me marcó, como ha sucedido con casi todos los escritores de mi generación en esta parte del mundo, pero no estaba pensando en los Buendía cuando escribí la historia de los Trueba' (*24*, p. 216). However, García Márquez is specifically mentioned in *Eva Luna* ('un bigotudo escritor colombiano en gira triunfal [...]', p. 224) and according to Gabrielle Colomines, Eva narrates to Rolf a little of the story of Aureliano of *Cien años de soledad* (*21*, p. 63). Traces of the master, if somewhat less direct, are similarly pervasive in *La casa*

---

[11] Quoted by Lucía Guerra Cunningham, *La narrativa de María Luisa Bombal: una visión de la existencia femenina*, Nova-Scholar (Madrid: Playor, 1980), p. 76.
[12] For an analysis of literary influence see Harold Bloom's outstanding study, *The Anxiety of Influence: A Theory of Poetry* (New York: Oxford University Press, 1973).

and justify investigation despite Marcela Coddou's opinion that the 'obsessive' critical urge to compare *La casa* with *Cien años de soledad* represents an attempt to 'discredit the originality and validity' of Allende's work (*18*, p. 26). Even critics favourable to Allende seek to unravel her literary relationship with García Márquez. While acknowledging the text's originality, Robert Antoni refers to a section of *La casa* which reads like pirated García Márquez (*7*, p. 21); Laurie Clancy says both that *La casa* is frequently dependent 'to the point of being parasitic' on García Márquez's text and that its coverage of the same terrain is 'both deliberate on the one hand, and intended to reinterpret and recover that terrain on the other' (*11*, pp. 29–30). Nicaslo Urbina attempts to demonstrate the direct influence of *Cien años de soledad* on *La casa* (*24*, p. 228).

The consensus of critical opinion is clearly that García Márquez has influenced Allende to a far greater extent than she is prepared to allow in her reference to García Márquez's general influence on writers of her generation (quoted above). Thematic and stylistic aspects of *La casa* recall *Cien años de soledad*: the broad historical sweep, the creation of cyclical mythic time, the urge to look beyond chronology towards temporal synchronicity at the end of both texts, the stylistic elaboration and profusion. More particularly, some of Allende's characters seem to be modelled on García Márquez's: José Arcadio's fascination with alchemy is matched by Marcos; Aureliano's fanaticism and solitude (though not his sense of futility) are reflected in Esteban Trueba, while his psychic powers, used to move objects and to predict the future, anticipate Clara's. Other characters in both texts share this power of clairvoyance: Pilar Ternera and Ursula (*Cien años de soledad*), the Mora sisters and Alba (*La casa*). The link between Remedios la Bella and Rosa is the strongest of all and the most frequently mentioned by critics, though it has been denied by Allende who claims that Rosa is based on a girlfriend her grandfather had once had: 'She really existed; she's not a copy from García Márquez as some people have said' (*2*, p. 42). If this is the case, the coincidence of independent character conception and development is unusual: of

Remedios the narrator states, 'no era un ser de este mundo' (*Cien años*, p. 310) while Rosa 'no era de este mundo' (12); also notable is Rosa's 'belleza de fondo de mar' (p. 35) which recalls the submarine splendour of Esteban of García Márquez's short story, 'El ahogado más hermoso del mundo'. Fraternal differences are similarly portrayed by both writers: on the one hand the outgoing and energetic brother (José Arcadio of *Cien años*, Nicolás of *La casa)*; on the other, the brother who is silent and withdrawn (Aureliano and Jaime). García Márquez's Amaranta, the embittered sister, corresponds to Férula whose death, surrounded by masks (146), recalls Fernanda's (*Cien años*, p. 498); the shipment of Marcos's coffin (25) recalls that of Fernanda's father, don Fernando, in *Cien años* (pp. 328–29). The infant Blanca and the ancient Ursula are linked through their miraculous reconciliation of extreme youth with extreme age: Ursula at her death looked like 'una anciana recién nacida' (*Cien años*, p. 470); Alba, for her part, displays a 'sabia expresión de ancianidad desde la cuna' (249). Ursula and Clara are strong women with the power to dominate men; both decide when to die and their houses fall into chaos and decline following their death (*Cien años*, pp. 460, 475; *La casa,* 275, 281). While García Márquez's Amaranta has incestuous relations with her nephew Aureliano José (*Cien años* p. 254), Allende's Jaime entertains incestuous though unfulfilled feelings for his niece, Alba (335).

In both novels, physical features and character traits are repeated down the generations (in *Cien años* Amaranta Úrsula combines the attributes of her great-great-grandmother Úrsula and her aunt, Remedios la Bella, p. 513; in *La casa* Alba inherits the green hair of her great aunt, Rosa, and the 'imaginación lunática' of her grandmother, Clara (286, 314). Among a host of lesser links one might mention the primitive remedies of Úrsula and Pedro García and popular fascination with the magical qualities of the magnet (*Cien años*, pp. 31, 79–80; *La casa*, 136, 135).

Allende's use of hyperbole is reminiscent of García Márquez's stylistic extravagances: Padre Nicanor's church, intended to be the biggest in the world (*Cien años,* p. 178), is echoed by Rosa's tablecloth, conceived as the largest in the world (13). While García

Márquez's Aureliano miraculously survives a 'carga de nuez vómica suficiente para matar a un caballo' (*Cien años,* p. 239), Rosa falls victim to 'suficiente veneno como para reventar a un toro' (33). If we extend our comparison to García Márquez's *El otoño del patriarca,* a similarity of stylistic structure emerges in the rapid alternation between first and third-person narrative which is used by both writers to convey the supreme political power of García Márquez's patriarch ('me quiten esta puerta de aquí y me la pongan allá, la quitaban, que me la vuelvan a poner, la ponían' [...]', *El otoño,* p. 16) and the seemingly supreme domestic power of Allende's Férula: 'póngame esto aquí, se lo ponían, cambien las flores de los jarrones, las cambiaban [...]' (101). Moreover, phrases which anticipate the future, such as 'muchos años después' and short Biblical confirmatory statements, such as 'así fue', are found throughout both *Cien años* and *La casa.*

Some of the parallels identified above indicate difference as well as coincidence, difference which relates, crucially, to gender. In Allende it is the female (Rosa) who is both inspired creator and sacrificial victim, the female (Férula) who wields unchallenged power. In *Cien años* the generations succeed each other by the patrilineal line and end in extinction; in *La casa,* descent is matrilineal and is still in progress at the close. García Márquez's treatment of his female characters is ambivalent: Úrsula plays a positive role in keeping her family in Macondo and curbing the excesses of her grandson, Arcadio, whom she herself replaces as governor (*Cien años,* pp. 204–06), but she is also cast in the role of stolid housewife who opposes the 'designios febriles' of her husband and struggles to uphold common-sensical principles (*Cien años,* pp. 95, 145–46).

In Allende's textual world, this scheme of things is inverted since conventional norms are generally supported by male characters — all Esteban wanted was 'un poco de normalidad' (211) and creative opposition to rigid practicality comes from women. The difference between Úrsula and Clara emerges in the distinct methods they employ to extend their houses: Ursula's carefully planned extensions (including 'una sala formal para las visitas' and 'un baño para las mujeres y otro para los hombres') reflect her own sense of practicality and order and her family's enhanced social status (146–47); Clara, on the other hand, makes ad hoc changes, knocking down walls and converting into a labyrinth her husband's domain, once ordered by strict hierarchical division, between the 'señorial prestancia' of the main residence and the disorder of the servants' quarters (43–44).[13] García Márquez's exuberant narrative lends tacit approval to the sexual excesses of both José Arcadio and Aureliano, the latter's mysterious aura enhanced by his detached promiscuity: 'las incontables mujeres que conoció en el desierto del amor, y que dispersaron su simiente en todo el litoral, no habían dejado rastro alguno en sus sentimientos' (*Cien años,* p. 282). In contrast, the comparable exploits of Esteban Trueba (of *La casa*) are described pejoratively, in terms of 'sembrando la región de bastardos' (67). It is the aristocratic Fernanda of *Cien años* who gives the most forthright expression to explicitly patriarchal values that go unchallenged by the text: 'tenía derecho a esperar un poco de más consideración de parte de su esposo, puesto que bien o mal era su cónyuge de sacramento, su autor, su legítimo perjudicador […]' (p. 449). Such submissiveness is not absent in *La casa,* but is presented as part of the peasant women's age-long social conditioning (rather than as the natural attribute of an upper-class female from the capital) and is challenged by Clara's progressive feminist views. As far as Remedios la Bella and Rosa are concerned, their ultimate destinies diverge just as strikingly as their corporeal lives coincide: the episode of Remedios's ascension to heaven (*Cien años,* p. 354) represents an implicitly male perspective and evokes the cult of *marianismo,* the idealized view of woman as semi-divine, pure and virginal.[14] There is no such good fortune for Rosa, whose

---

[13] Francine Masiello points out that in the feminine novel 'the house is dismantled to indicate the potential freedom of woman and her opposition to the state': 'Texto, ley, transgresión: especulación sobre la novela (feminista) de vanguardia', *Revista Iberoamericana,* 51 (1985), 807–22 (p. 813).

[14] For an account of *marianismo* see Evelyn P. Stevens, 'Marianismo: the Other Face of Machismo in Latin America', in *Female and Male in Latin America,* ed. by Ann Pescatello (Pittsburgh: Pittsburgh University Press, 1973), pp. 89–101.

body, despite its supernatural beauty — preserved for a time by embalming — eventually proves mortal and dissolves into 'un polvillo tenue y gris' (290).

Critics such as Hutcheon have noted that feminists — as well as other 'ex-centric' writers — both depend upon and challenge, through parody, male traditions in art.[15] The similarities between the novels are so close as to make almost compelling the charge of plagiarism, frequently levelled at Allende. Rather than a positive (feminist) remoulding of *Cien años*, *La casa* is seen as recycling themes and techniques already perfected by García Márquez. But it is clear from the examples cited above that Allende's text displays both unconscious imitation and conscious recasting, in almost equal measure. The newborn Blanca may recall the monster with the pig's tail, feared as the curse of incestuous union in *Cien años*, but she matures into an almost beautiful girl 'que no se parecía en nada al armadillo que era cuando nació' (102). *La casa* is ultimately a tale of hope, that develops, somewhat against the odds, from unpromising beginnings in austere patriarchal rule. *Cien años* follows a radically different trajectory, moving from the apparent paradise of the newly established Macondo (p. 90) to the final destruction of the town and the extinction of the Buendías. Allende's Mr Brown, an unmistakable parody of his namesake in *Cien años*, is summoned to tackle a plague of ants at *Las Tres Marías*, but his ponderous methods prove ineffective and he is upstaged by the old peasant Pedro García. García Márquez's Mr Brown, on the other hand, works for the banana company that forces capitalist modernization on the town, exploiting without restraint both natural and human resources and ruining Macondo in the process. Allende subordinates foreign expertise to superior indigenous knowledge and humiliates the *gringo*; García Márquez can only lament the irresistible force of *gringo* intervention in indigenous affairs and the humiliation of the townspeople.

---

[15] For further discussion of this topic, see Linda Hutcheon, *A Poetics of Postmodernism: History, Theory, Fiction* (London: Routledge, 1988), p. 134.

The range and frequency of the thematic and technical parallels between *La casa* and *Cien años* demonstrate beyond reasonable doubt Allende's considerable debt to García Márquez but comparison of the two texts also highlights an aspect of this literary relationship that has attracted less critical attention — Allende's creative divergences from García Márquez: her parodic inversions of his patriarchal discourse, and her more subtle inflections of his master's voice with her unobtrusive, yet insistently feminine, intonations. Shaw points out that what makes *La casa* 'a genuinely "inaugural" novel' is its 'strong presentation of women and of the way they have been able to empower themselves over the period of time covered by the novel' (*22*, p. 58).

3. The Sociopolitical Dimension

When *La casa* is set alongside *Cien años*, it becomes evident that Allende deals with history in a way different from that adopted by García Márquez, and a brief comparison will help to pinpoint certain essential and characteristic features of Allende's text. García Márquez combines an omniscient narrative perspective with a fictionalized presentation of history. Allende, on the other hand, consciously undermines omniscient narration since Esteban's contributions to the narrative often diverge from the view presented by Alba.[16]

In *Cien años* García Márquez mounts an effective challenge to official versions of events such as the Colombian banana strike of 1928, though by no means from a position of historical authority, since he believes that history cannot be factual, being recuperable only through fiction. The number of people killed in that strike — given as three thousand by a survivor, José Arcadio Segundo (p. 432) — is deliberately exaggerated in *Cien años*, but the text's crushing repudiation of the official silence and denial that had enveloped the issue ('En Macondo no ha pasado nada [...]. Este es un pueblo feliz', p. 434) is hardly diminished as a result.

Allende's perspective of events in Chile is inevitably different: their recent ocurrence, their lingering effects, and the personal tragedy inflicted on the author herself account for the testimonial flavour of the final chapters. But her work also moves away from

---

[16] Alba's doubts about the existence of her putative father, Jean de Satigny (409), may be seen as an implicit expression of female independence and a mocking repudiation of Freudian oedipal theory. In addition, however, it points to Alba's uncertainty as narrator and recalls popular doubts about Colonel Aureliano Buendía's existence at the end of *Cien años*, doubts significantly not shared by Gabriel (representing García Márquez) who was certain of his existence (p. 526).

plain historical documentary, though not in the same direction as García Márquez's. *La casa* itself contributes to the perpetuation of her uncle's legacy, and in representing his words (349), helps keep them in circulation.[17] Though a condensed version of Salvador Allende's final radio address reproduces verbatim some of the phrases used by the President, its purity as a piece of historical documentation is compromised by its insertion into a magical realist text.[18] The president's heroic words — 'pagaré con mi vida la lealtad del pueblo. Siempre estaré junto a ustedes [...]' (349) — are tinged by the discourse of the supernatural which surround them. His promise to be with his people following his death recalls Clara's assurance that she will return, since her passing 'no sería una separación, sino una forma de estar más unidas' (275). Salvador Allende's heroism also relates to the heightened emotions and exaggerated character traits found in the fiction, so that while the magical realist context colours history, removing it from the level of bleak reality in which it seemed submerged at that point, historical discourse, for its part, confers some anchorage in reality for the narration of seemingly unreal events surrounding it. The magical and the real interrelate explicitly in the military's attempts to rewrite history and reconstruct geography (362–63; see p. 70, below).[19] García Márquez deliberately overstates the death toll in the 1928 banana strike; Allende moves away from authoritative historical writing by infecting the real with the magical, and vice-versa, conferring literary force on what might at first appear to be plain historical discourse.

In *La casa*, Allende treats fact and fiction, reality and myth on an equal footing: thus real historical characters such as Salvador

---

[17] Santiago Colás (*27*, p. 134) points out that the *cita* is a marker of temporal distance, of the absence of the past; but it also brings the disappeared past or individual back, (re)presenting them and sending their silenced messages back into circulation.

[18] The full text of President Allende's last radio broadcast to the nation may be found in Joan E. Garcés, *Allende y la experiencia chilena* (Barcelona: Ariel, 1976), pp. 391–92.

[19] Antoni disregards this link when he states that at the end of *La casa*, 'there is no longer magic but only realism' (*7*, p. 21).

Allende and Pablo Neruda share the same reality as unreal characters such as Esteban Trueba and Alba.[20] Here Allende displays her affinity with New Historical writing, marked — as Seymour Menton points out — by the novelistic interaction of historical and fictional characters (*32*, p. 23). Allende as post-modernist writer has drawn limited — and often qualified — critical acknowledgement (*38*, p. 16), but an obvious postmodernist trait is her foregrounding of the female voice, which consistently undermines patriarchal values and, by extension, a monological conception of the world based on rigid binary divisions.

Further postmodernist features of *La casa* are its metafictional commentary on its own construction, its problematization of the narrative by its thematic duplications and cyclical patterns, and its subversion of narrative authority by manipulating diverse narrative discourses vying for supremacy. All this suggests the text's strong postmodernist pedigree — despite its lack of those flamboyant but now overfamiliar techniques such as alternative endings (John Fowles, *The French Lieutenant's Woman*) and the textualization of the reader (Italo Calvino, *If on a Winter's Night*).[21] However, considered in terms of McHale's identification of postmodernist fiction as, above all, 'illusion-breaking art', *La casa* fails to meet the requirements for inclusion in the postmodern category.[22] Despite the text's often playful juxtaposition of various levels of reality, Allende

---

[20] A third historical figure associated with the Left, the songwriter and theatrical director, Víctor Jara, who was executed after the coup, is not mentioned in *La casa*. However, he may have served to inspire, at least in part, Allende's portrayal of Pedro Tercero García. For further discussion of this point see *15*, pp. 98–110.

[21] From the technical point of view Allende's texts may well appear unambitious, but it is well to bear in mind the following point made by Terry Eagleton: 'It is unwise to assume that ambiguity, indeterminacy, undecidability are always subversive strikes against an arrogantly monological certitude; on the contrary, they are the stock-in-trade of many a juridical enquiry and official investigation'; *The Ideology of the Aesthetic* (Oxford: Basil Blackwell, 1990), pp. 379–80.

[22] Brian McHale, *Postmodernist Fiction* (London: Methuen, 1987), p. 221. McHale refers to several Latin American literary examples in his extensive survey.

does not deliberately and consistently point to the artificiality of her textual world or to the slippery elusiveness of language (although she does exult in what she sees as its magical possibilities, as we shall see). Although some elements of realist representation — what McHale terms 'aboutness' (p. 221) — linger in the most radically anti-mimetic texts, in *La casa* 'what happens' is of great importance — as might be expected of a writer best known for her traditional story-telling powers. Furthermore, as a fervent feminist and socialist, she is more interested in finding the most accessible and forceful artistic expression for her first-hand experiences than in indulging in detached, philosophical game-playing or technical *tours de force*. Here she may be aligned with those Post-Boom writers who tread, as Shaw points out, 'an uneasy path between the Barthes-*Tel Quel*-Sarduyian notion that the text can have no exterior referent and the old-fashioned idea that the relationship between signifier and signified is completely unproblematic' (*22*, p. 57).

Allende's background in journalism is also significant in this context, since the journalist's main objective is usually to convey information using language as a natural medium rather than investigating the limits of its communicative powers. In writing *La casa*, Allende does not problematize the 'metalanguages' of freedom, justice, and truth but takes these traditional topics with full seriousness.[23] Owing to the weakness of journalism in Latin America, narrative fiction has often been obliged to assume greater responsibility in this area than it might have otherwise; even today most writers in Latin America are judged by the social effectiveness of their work. [24]

---

[23] Arguing against those who proclaim the exhaustion of the old discourses of reason, truth, freedom, and subjectivity, Eagleton affirms that 'it is unlikely that a politics which does not take these traditional topics with full seriousness will prove resourceful and resilient enough to oppose the arrogance of power'; *The Ideology of the Aesthetic*, p. 415.

[24] 'Latin American intellectuals have frequently emphasized the ideological dimension of literature, even going so far as to consider formal and stylistic brilliance as "ancillary", or instrumental and secondary, with respect to the political and social content.' See Amaryll Chanady, 'The Territorialization

We shall here examine this sociopolitical aspect of *La casa* without, however, losing sight of the text's postmodernist qualities. In his study of the relation between journalism and Latin American narrative, Aníbal González argues that journalism has served to demystify writing and the notion of 'literature' itself; and the dual affiliation of many writers encourages them to inhabit the margins, finding maximum creative freedom in the 'gray no-man's land between discourses' (*28*, p. 14). It is in this indeterminate area that we shall later locate Allende's peculiar brand of postmodernism.

La casa is a long and multi-faceted text, thematically complicated and structurally intricate. It is, however, realist to the extent that extratextual references take priority over metafictional aspects. Many themes are treated, but of central importance, and impinging on most others, is that of injustice, which derives from the patriarchal organization of society and emerges most blatantly in class and gender relations. Patriarchy is a historical creation, matured over two thousand five hundred years; the term describes 'the relationship of a dominant [male] group, considered superior, to a subordinate group, considered inferior, in which the dominance is mitigated by mutual obligations and reciprocal rights' (*43*, p. 217). Victims as well as beneficiaries colluded in its creation: women, belonging in general to the former category, as well as men, belonging to the latter; peasants and the urban under-classes, as well as the privileged land-owning or entrepreneurial minorities. Marginalized groups collude in their own exclusion from wealth and power, partly because of the deep-seatedness of patriarchal values, many of which are reinforced by Biblical sanction: the basic unit of patriarchal organization is the family, where, according to Saint Paul, the husband is the head and the wife's natural role is that of passive and compliant helpmeet (Ephesians 5.23). If both men and women have suffered discrimination owing to their lowly social class, poor working-class women suffer doubly, under the yoke of both social exploitation and sexual oppression. Such a patently unjust system is

---

of the Imaginary in Latin America: Self-Affirmation and Resistance to Metropolitan Paradigms,' in *31*, pp.125–44 (pp.136–37).

accepted because it is almost universally seen as natural, eternal, unchanging, divinely ordained.

The patriarchal system ranges not only male against female but also class against class in its apportionment of dominance and subjection in society. Esteban García is cast in the mould of a fiery Old Testament patriarch through his moral posturing and his uncompromising defence of the status quo. Dominated in his youth by his sister Férula, he breaks free of her (49) and begins afresh in the role of tyrant rather than victim; he justifies his conduct by appealing to ingrained human inequality — 'no es cuestión de ricos y pobres, sino de fuertes y débiles' (134). A jealous guardian of his own class interests, he develops a fine sensitivity to any perceived threat to them. He will not tolerate the slightest challenge to his authority (67) and is merciless in his treatment of political opponents such as Pedro Tercero García whom he punishes for seeking to raise political awareness among his *inquilinos* (150). When his estate is returned to him by the military government following its expropriation by the previous socialist régime, he exacts terrible revenge on his tenants (365–66); in recounting the episode to the prostitute, Tránsito Soto, he specifically casts himself in the role of father who punishes, then forgives, his children when they return to him: 'algún día volverán y no me quedará más remedio que tenderles una mano, son como niños [...]' (397).

It is true that Esteban makes some significant attempts to improve the lot of his *inquilinos*: he builds a school and offers instruction on diet and current affairs. But he ensures that the social order will not be undermined in the process: 'no era partidario de que adquirieran otros conocimientos para que no se les llenara la cabeza con ideas inapropiadas a su estado y condición' (64). Any such fears which Esteban has appear to be misplaced, since the misery of the peasants is centuries-old and has come to be seen by everyone, including the peasants themselves, as the natural order of things. The state of affairs which Esteban finds when he first returns to *Las Tres Marías* — described by the woodcutter Esteban meets as 'una tierra de nadie, un roquerío sin ley' (53) — underlines what Gabriela

Mistral calls Chile's 'rural barbarism'.[25] A suckling infant sleeps with a puppy in a box lined with newspaper; a retarded youth is tied by the neck to a post and left naked to drool and rave, beating his outsized sex organ against the ground in a primitive gesture of protest; an old woman, whose bones have emerged through the sores in her back, has endured a slow death for four years (63).

Physical suffering is complemented by mental torpor: Esteban finds that the peasants cannot conceive of small maps representing large areas of the world and that they have no knowledge of events beyond their immediate environment (65). *La casa* also offers portraits of urban squalor, for example the 'conventillo' where Férula spends her last days (145), and the equally depressed area where Jaime's surgery is located (228). Such human misery might appear to confirm Esteban's simple theory about the natural division of human beings into strong and weak; and the acceptance by the weak of the patriarchal system which works so patently to their disadvantage might point to the virtual impossibility of change. Thus his foreman, Pedro Segundo, is as convinced as Esteban that social inequality is a 'ley de Dios' (158) and he cannot conceive of his son's relationship with Blanca 'porque esa posibilidad no estaba en el orden natural del mundo' (168). Nana, the long-serving family servant, shares this view and resents Pedro Tercero's breach of class proprieties: 'Aprende, mocoso, a meterte con los de tu clase y no con señoritas' (150). It is this 'unnatural' relationship which provokes Esteban to violence not only against Pedro Tercero, whom he tries to kill, but also against his wife and daughter, who never really forgive him for it.

Esteban's inflexible and reactionary attitude to gender relations is clearly in keeping with his views on social class and the link between them appears clearly on several occasions. He classifies women according to simple categories: 'en mi generación hacíamos un distingo entre las mujeres decentes y las otras y también dividíamos a las decentes entre propias y ajenas' (29). He also

---

[25] Quoted by Frederick B. Pike, 'The Background for Reform in Chile', in *Latin America: A Historical Reader*, ed. by Lewis Hanke (Boston: Little, Brown, 1974), pp. 655–67 (p. 662).

identifies the clear class-based division between women who are
available for passing sexual gratification (Pancha and others of her
class) and those who are suitable for marriage (70). Men are also
categorized by class: as a peasant, Pedro Segundo is not a suitable
companion for Esteban (65). But the lot of peasant women is far
worse: not only do they suffer economic discrimination in relation to
their male counterparts — for example, they are denied bonus
payments (64) — but they are also the defenceless victims of random
sexual exploitation. Patriarchal gender-attitudes — like those relating
to class — perpetuate themselves effortlessly since they too have
been internalized by exploiters and exploited alike.

Women of all classes are affected — though in varying degrees
— ranging from Esteban's sister Férula to Pancha, his peasant lover,
rejected when she becomes pregnant. Férula shares her brother's bad
temper but, as a woman, is obliged to repress it (48). Constrained by
her gender to sacrifice her life to care for her ailing mother, she tells
Esteban that she would have liked to have been born a man (50). The
position of Pancha is obviously worse, since her lowly social status
leaves her open to sexual exploitation by Esteban. Just as Pedro
Segundo accepted social inequality, so Pancha and other women of
her class accept their sexual subordination 'por la costumbre
ancestral de todas las mujeres de su estirpe de bajar la cabeza ante el
macho' (62). Patriarchal values are inbred and seemingly
unquestioned by the victim. Esteban himself meets any challenge to
his rapacious activities with violence: like an all-powerful
nineteenth-century *cacique*, he is able to kill social inferiors with
impunity (67), and his violence, in attempting to thwart Pedro
Tercero's 'intrusion' (through Blanca) into a higher social class,
follows the same pattern of behaviour.

While peasant women can be used and discarded at will,
women belonging to the higher classes are treated with more respect,
since they form part of a contract between males, being — as
Esteban puts it — either 'propias' or 'ajenas' (29). When Esteban
asks Severo whether he has any marriageable daughters (following
the death of Rosa, to whom Esteban was engaged), the older man
shows a kind of commercial honesty in disclosing his daughter's

defects (90), but Esteban is unperturbed, since they will not affect her principal, utilitarian value — the production of healthy legitimate children. Later, following her marriage to Jean de Satigny, arranged by her father, Blanca realizes that she is part of a deal struck between the two men (235): Satigny's stake is purely financial, since he is not interested in normal marital relations with Blanca (235), while Esteban's interest relates to saving appearances by marrying his daughter, pregnant by her peasant lover, Pedro Tercero, to an aristocratic pretender.

Social change appears to be a remote prospect in view of both the widespread acceptance of patriarchal values, and the machinations of the unscrupulously powerful to restore order when the system is threatened. Despite her passion for Pedro Tercero, Blanca's distaste for his lifestyle (296) may suggest that class divisions are ultimately stronger than love, and cannot be suppressed. On the political front too, it seems that fear and resignation will always combine to prevent change: 'el zorro siempre acaba por comerse a las gallinas' (185). The forces ranged in favour of continuity are formidable; none the less the society depicted here is far from stable, and the long-standing patriarchal system is under clear threat. Change is indeed pervasive and unstoppable — at both local and national levels: the arrival of modernity is represented by the motor car (Severo del Valle is the country's first car owner, 118) and the telephone (160). On the economic front, the payment of Esteban's workers in cash removes the old semifeudal system of estate bonds (172) — a change instigated by Clara, who had previously warned her husband: 'no puedes impedir que el mundo cambie [...]' (164). On the national political level, change comes most spectacularly in the defeat of 'los de siempre' in the 1970 elections — which may be seen as the culmination of several local expressions of resistance, not least that embodied in old Pedro García's fable about the hens uniting to defeat the fox (137).

Women represent the most potent threat to the patriarchal system, despite having internalized (in many cases) its most reactionary values. Férula generally proves herself to be a staunch defender of the system, thereby living up to her name: like Nana, she does not see Pedro Tercero as a suitable companion for Blanca: 'era el colmo que la niña no tuviera alguien de su clase con quien mezclarse [...]' (107); her meetings with the peasant women at *Las Tres Marías* serve to reinforce the status quo by their exclusive focus on religious ritual (105). In these respects, she is as much a pillar of the patriarchal order as Esteban himself; but she steps outside its strict precepts in her unwomanly domination of the young Esteban, suggesting that she has, to some extent, assumed the role of the man she had always wanted to be (50). She steps well outside its confines when this assumed masculine role colours the intensity of her feelings for Clara — feelings more appropriate in a husband than a sister-in-law (124) — and leads to her resentment of her brother as a rival for Clara's affections and to his expulsion of her with the violent fury of a man dealing with his wife's seducer (129). Férula infringes patriarchal norms which exclude deviant relations between females.[26] She sees herself as a sinner rather than a rebel and confesses her improper feelings for Clara to her priest (100). If Férula's name suggests rigid conformity, those of the four main female characters (Nívea, Clara, Blanca, Alba) signify the coming of the light, an end to the dark age of female subservience.

Allende's women are uncontaminated by the conditioning of patriarchy and the centuries-old blindness afflicting their gender. They are a kind of *tabula rasa*, receptive to new experience. Allende explains the significance of the names as follows:

> Quise simbolizar un estado de pureza, pero no la pureza entendida como virginidad, como normalmente se entiende en la mujer, sino que es la pureza para enfrentar el mundo con ojos nuevos, no contaminados, sin prejuicios, abiertos, tolerantes, y un alma capaz de impactarse con los colores del mundo, por eso es que no tienen color [...] (*5*, p. 12).

---

[26] 'Strong attachments between women, disinclining them to heterosexual marriage, are recognized as far more dangerous to the patriarchal foundation of society than any amount of campaigning against specific inequalities'; Pam Morris, *Literature and Feminism*, p. 39.

It is perhaps significant that two Chilean examples of early socialist newspapers with an explicitly feminist orientation were *La Aurora* and *La Alborada*. 'Women', as Asunción Lavrin points out, 'especially in the early 1910s, were regarded as still immature, in need of light to reveal the possibilities that centuries of darkness and oppression had hidden. Awakening, seeing the light, were frequent metaphors in the writings of the Left' (*42*, p. 523). In contrast with Férula and her religious obfuscations, Clara attempts to lighten the darkness of the peasant women, who regard masculine violence not only as normal but as a sign of love (105–06). Such attitudes lingered in Chile longer than elsewhere; domestic violence was not made a crime until 1990 (*39*, p. 89).

Clara is, of course, perpetuating the feminist interests of her mother, Nívea, who was indifferent to religion, but dedicated to the cause of female suffrage (11). Nívea's feminist credentials also emerge in her abolition of old family tradition by cutting down the poplar tree (82) while Clara establishes her feminist pedigree as a child, when she questions Padre Restrepo about the existence of hell, thereby undermining the masculine and authoritarian discourse of official religion (14). Taking advantage of one of the priest's theatrical pauses, Clara questions the very basis of his doctrine, unconsciously mocking his high Biblical rhetoric by her spontaneous recourse to the low language of the street: '¡Pst! ¡Padre Restrepo! Si el cuento del infierno fuera pura mentira, nos chingamos todos...' (14). Her speaking out both violates the priest's rhetorical silence and, more seriously, contravenes the Pauline doctrine that women be silent in church (I Corinthians 14.34). This is the most blatant and memorable rebuttal of patriarchal thinking in the text, and contrasts sharply with the unquestioning assimilation of such assumptions elsewhere. As Gerda Lerner suggests: 'to step outside of patriarchal thought means: being skeptical to every known system of thought; being critical of all assumptions, ordering values and definitions' (*43*, p. 228).

Clara's attitude to the Church coincides with Nívea's but her vision of society and the remedies it requires is sharper than her mother's: she perceives the unbridgeable distance between the naive political enthusiasm of her mother's middle-class circle and the languid resignation of the peasant women and realizes that charity is wholly inappropriate to tackle such monumental injustice (83). Despite her own notorious lack of practical sense, Clara teaches the peasant women how to boil milk, treat diarrhoea, and bleach clothes (105). Her work recalls Latin American feminists' concern during the early part of this century with public health issues. Clara's silences, however, might appear rather negative: she speaks to no one for nine years after Rosa's death (45) and refuses to speak to Esteban after he strikes her (192). Her first long silence underlines her anarchic character: she speaks in church when she should have remained silent, and remains silent when she is expected to speak.

Her silence may be seen as a response to the male violation of her sister's body — an experience which cannot be spoken about. Clara feels partly responsible for her sister's fate since she had foreseen a death in the family. She regains her voice to announce that she is marrying Esteban — thereby expiating after a fashion her sin against Rosa, by marrying, in her place, a man she does not love. Her voluntary silence reproduces the deathly silence of Rosa who is present in body but absent in spirit for the doctor and his assistant, just as Clara's later silence towards Esteban removes her from him while she remains physically present. Clara reacts with silence following the shock of seeing her sister's body violated during the course of a procedure which is stereotypically masculine in its desire to uncover the secret of the female: 'procedieron a hurgar en la intimidad de la bella Rosa [...]' (35); later she reacts in a similar way when Esteban assaults her, conduct which is also stereotypically masculine in its force and violence. Here Clara turns on its head the conventional view of silence as a peculiarly female virtue, signifying submissiveness and conformity, by using it as a weapon, first against her family and society, both implicated in her eyes in the death and violation of her sister, and then against Esteban, plunging him into new depths of solitude. Loneliness, most often the lot of the neglected wife, is visited instead upon the husband. Beyond this, Clara's silence may be seen as a symbolic withdrawal from language which, like her sister's body, is heavily inscribed by masculinity.

Clara communicates with Blanca before her daughter is born, 'en un diálogo secreto y constante con la criatura' (101) — presumably by pre-linguistic semiotic means, of the kind explored by Kristeva.[27]

Blanca's contribution to the feminist cause takes the form of breaching social conventions rather than firm political commitment. Uninhibited by moral or social constraints, she sleeps with the peasant, Pedro Tercero, becomes a single mother after the break-up of her short-lived marriage to Jean de Satigny, and maintains her unorthodox propensities well into adulthood, recoiling from marriage partly because of the loss of status it would imply, but also to indulge her liking for the illicit and unsanctified (295). Her rejection of marriage is significant since it is an institution seen by feminists as the pillar of the patriarchal system, facilitating the perpetuation of masculine power and the confinement of women to the private domestic space.[28]

Alba, like her mother, is not politically committed: she feels that she could give her life for a good cause (303), but unlike her lover Miguel, she lacks ideological conviction. It is she, however, who raids her family's stockpiles of food and weapons so that the poor can be fed and the revolutionaries armed, and it is she who pays the terrible cost in terms of imprisonment, humiliation, and torture, for sheltering fugitives after the military coup. It is no coincidence that the help she receives comes from a series of women: the spirit of her grandmother Clara instills in her the will to live; Ana Díaz, Miguel's militant colleague during the student sit-in, comforts her in prison; the prostitute, Tránsito Soto, secures her release; and the

---

[27] For a useful summary of the semiotic see Elizabeth Grosz, *Sexual Subversions: Three French Feminists* (St Leonards, NSW: Allen and Unwin, 1989), p. 43, and Paul Julian Smith, *The Body Hispanic: Gender and Sexuality in Spanish and Spanish American Literature* (Oxford: Clarendon Press, 1989), p. 18.

[28] 'Feminism has specifically marked out the institution of marriage as the pillar of the patriarchal system, a crucial instance of the exchange of women which still ensures masculine power and represents a fundamental crux in women's oppression.' See Rosi Braidotti, *Patterns of Dissonance: A Study of Women in Contemporary Philosophy*, trans. by Elizabeth Guild (Cambridge: Polity Press, 1991), p. 180.

anonymous downtrodden woman (representing unsung female virtue) gives her shelter and arranges for her to be taken home. Such female resilience and solidarity not only secure survival in the face of the worst militaristic excesses of the patriarchal system, but anticipate eventual victory over it: 'Entonces supe que el coronel García y otros como él tienen sus días contados, porque no han podido destruir el espíritu de esas mujeres' (408).

Tránsito Soto and Pancha García deserve further mention as women who, in different ways, show independence of spirit and refusal to comply with social expectations. In Tránsito, a prostitute, one might expect to find a resigned and vulnerable figure, representing woman as sexual commodity who exists only to satisfy male desire. But Tránsito, against the odds, has shaped a life of enterprise and vigour, maintaining her independence from male predators and pimps, but at the same time rejecting capitalist indivi-dualism in favour of a cooperative organization of her business (116–17). As a prostitute, Tránsito is a marginal figure in society; as a literary character, she plays a marginal role in this text; but despite her marginality it is she who secures Alba's release and without her, the narrative would not have been written (117). She represents — as her name 'Tránsito' suggests — the continuing trajectory of woman from the margins towards the centre and from subjection towards freedom.

Pancha García's life moves in a similar direction: a peasant girl who is sexually exploited by Esteban, her seemingly ingrained submissiveness is displaced by lethal purpose as she primes her grandson, Esteban García, to avenge Esteban Trueba's neglect, reminding him incessantly of his blood relationship with the *patrón* (270). Like Tránsito, Pancha appears to be marginal, one of the scores of peasant women ravished by Esteban, condemned already by her gender and her class. She too, however, moves from the margins by inspiring hatred and resentment in Esteban García, the issue (at one remove) of that 'enorme envase' (66), her swollen body that had so repelled Esteban. Her grandson, whose natural place in both the social and textual scheme of things would be well inside the margins, moves to centre stage in both spheres through the torture he inflicts on Alba, one of the central characters. Just as the writing of the text depends on the will of a character (Tránsito Soto) who flits in and out of the story without seeming to leave much trace, so its culminating episodes, which reaffirm female power through the survival of Alba and the feminized figure of Esteban Trueba, derive their origins from a contrary emotional force, represented by the almost forgotten, embittered character of Pancha García.

That women are not idealized is clear from Allende's portrait of Blanca. It is true that her pottery classes cater for mongols as well as young ladies (255) and that her creative abilities recall Rosa's (167), but her outlook is rather narrow — she has no interest in events in Europe, for example (173) — and her personal happiness and comfort take priority over the wellbeing of others. At the time of the food shortages (under the Allende régime) she hoards (332), and after the coup, when supplies are plentiful but expensive, she revels in her purchasing power (353). Rather than contribute like Alba to the Church-sponsored programme of feeding needy children, Blanca withdraws into a private world of lethargy and self-pity (360). She finally leaves the country with Pedro Tercero to live in relative comfort and safety in Canada (379).

Allende does not overlook the female opponents of the socialist régime who contributed critically to its defeat: 'las mujeres de la oposición [...] desfilaban por las calles aporreando sus cacerolas en protesta por el desabastecimiento' (343). The first women's demonstration against Salvador Allende took place as early as December 1971 and as Mattelart states, 'they all had as their common thematic symbol and noisy showpiece a pot, which the women would beat with a lid or spoon'.[29] This movement, known as 'El Poder Femenino', brought together women with vested interests, the wives of the striking truck-drivers, the wives of policemen and of members of the armed forces. Such women did not suffer: they

---

[29] Michelle Mattelart, 'Chile: The Feminine Version of the Coup d'état', in *Sex and Class in Latin America*, ed. by June Nash and Helen Icken Safa (New York: Praeger, 1976), pp. 279–301 (p. 282).

hoarded (like Blanca) and profited from the hardships exacerbated by their own actions. Their influence, channelled via grass-roots organizations, such as the 'centros de madres', was built on their insistent claim that family life was being undermined by socialism. In this way they assumed an aura of sanctity, and succeeded in concealing their real motivation, the defence of their class interests. They did not stop short of using 'macho semantics' (Mattelart, p. 296) and effectively coerced men, and in particular the armed forces, into action. Women had certainly broken out of the domestic space but it was, ironically, to help steer the country towards repression and state terror. With the violent reassertion of rigid patriarchal principles following the coup, women were relegated to a totally passive role and El Poder Femenino was dismantled.

Thus the role of women in recent Chilean history has been negative as well as positive; in *La casa* the generous and progressive spirit of Alba must be set against the impoverished and backward-looking qualities of Férula; against the commitment and resilience of Ana Díaz, devoted to the cause of collective well-being, must be placed the narrow search for personal happiness represented by Blanca. The role of the Left has also been problematic and Allende does not ignore the disunity which contributed to the fall of the Unidad Popular government: Jaime, Alba's uncle, who works selflessly as a doctor for the victims of oppression, resents the extremism of Alba's lover, Miguel, which he believes to be more harmful to the government than the machinations of the Right. Miguel is portrayed as the left-wing equivalent of Esteban, opposing his reactionary views but sharing his undemocratic, reactionary methods: '[...] la revolución no se podía hacer desde las urnas electorales, sino con la sangre del pueblo' (318). Rejecting out of hand the possibility of peaceful change, Miguel remains 'fiel a su teoría de que a la violencia de los ricos había que oponer la violencia del pueblo' (375). Both he and Esteban are locked in a cycle of violence, blind to the spirit of reconciliation championed by Alba, who suffers far more than either of them, but still retains her faith in the possibility of a different future, built on peace and forgiveness.

Unlike Miguel, Esteban does eventually begin to see the light. (Ultra-Leftism has been identified by several historians as a major factor in Salvador Allende's downfall: see, for example, *44*, p. 307.)

The Left is also shown to share some of those patriarchal prejudices normally associated with their political opponents: the student sit-in is supported by a left-wing lecturer, Sebastián Gómez, who is unsympathetic towards Alba when she is indisposed: 'Esto pasa por meter a las mujeres en cosas de hombres' (308). For Gómez, Marxist action is a male activity; for Miguel (ironically, in view of Alba's subsequent suffering) the guerrilla struggle has no place for 'una mujer enamorada' (377). Eagleton has identified sexism as structural to Marxism which, he claims, bears the imprint of the virile Western male (*The Ideology of the Aesthetic*, p. 221). The Chilean Left was certainly not immune to misogynistic prejudice, as evidenced by their silence on the military junta's retrogressive policy towards women (*38*, p. 75).

Isabel Allende's treatment of feminism and socialism seeks to highlight the complexities and nuances of their recent political postures that may underpin her refusal to contemplate an unproblematic future. Critics such as Gabriela Mora object to what they see as the negative conclusion of the novel in which the impersonal forces of destiny appear to overshadow human efforts to institute social change (*20*, pp. 55–57). Certainly Allende does appear to see history as cyclical, and her text is marked by repetition. Alba's recent experiences and her sensitivity to the limits of human knowledge and understanding inevitably reinforce her sense of recurrent suffering, and lower her expectations of a different future. On the other hand, her faith in the resilience of the female spirit is manifest in her own inclination towards reconciliation rather than revenge, a choice which points to escape from cyclic violence. Alba's view of Chilean history is almost identical to the view of more general human history expressed by Eagleton, whose Marxist ideology does not seek to underestimate human limitations: 'So far nothing particularly special has occurred: history to date has simply been the same old story, a set of variations on persisting structures of oppression and exploitation' (*The Ideology of the Aesthetic*, p. 215). Alba's view of a problematic reality commands more respect than the idealistic faith in revolution of her lover Miguel who is prepared to use the methods of his opponents to achieve his ends, even suggesting to Alba that one day he may kill her grandfather (376). Gabriela Mora objects to Alba's final mood of resignation as she waits for the return of Miguel and for better times. But 'tiempos mejores' are also expected by the firebrand Miguel (377), whose weaknesses hardly include passivity. Though Mora, in her somewhat negative study of Allende's work, may be right in principle when she claims that feminist activity should not be restricted to writing and waiting, her strictures seem rather out of place in view of Alba's pregnancy and her generous contribution to the struggle against dictatorship. While Alba is ignorant of the paternity of the child she is carrying, she is — significantly — certain of its gender ('hija de tantas violaciones, o tal vez hija de Miguel, pero sobre todo hija mía'; 411). The female line, representing the most potent agent of change, is set to continue.

It might be argued that, far from being passive, Alba embodies the woman who is outside the control of patriarchy, freely choosing, rather than being forced by destiny, to repeat the feminist defiance expressed by her forbears: in her writing (a suspect occupation for a woman) she follows Clara; as a single mother she will emulate Blanca.

La casa bears powerful testimony to the sociopolitical history of twentieth-century Chile. In this respect it has much in common with testimonial writing which, as its name suggests, focuses on historical fact and largely eschews formal and technical experimentation which might compromise its prime purpose of conveying a political message. Allende's achievement is to offer a penetrating historical analysis which is enhanced rather than diminished by her use of artistic techniques such as magical realism. Her vision, in keeping with the tendency of Post-Boom writing towards 'modified optimism' (*22*, p. 69), is ultimately hopeful and positive: she locates the possibility of change not in the blinkered fanaticism of certain sections of the Left but rather in the wider appreciation of the more spiritual female virtues which might serve as a necessary counterweight to the increasingly exclusive male values of reason and logic. Allende proposes greater space for alternative, often incompatible, values — intuition, myth, magic — which relate to ancient human bonds with the natural world.

4. Magical Realism, Myth and Carnival

The previous chapter focused on the sociohistorical aspects of *La casa* — aspects which seem to be at odds with the illusion-breaking thrust of postmodernism — and pointed to the text's affinity with testimonial writing. According to Jean Franco, this genre 'covers a spectrum between autobiography and oral history' and implies 'a subject as witness to and participant in public events' (*34*, p. 71). It is significant that the spirit of Clara, which visits Alba following her ordeal at the hands of Esteban García, urges her to write a testimony recording the suffering that she and others had been forced to endure (391). The text, as *testimonio*, is strongly inflected by feminist perspectives, exemplifying that *concienciación* that occurs once women transgress the boundaries of domestic space (*33*, p. 71). However, the testimonial mode of narration is underpinned by such concepts as truth, clarity, and meaning, by an authoritative sense of rigour and purpose. In *La casa*, the interaction of such sobriety with the equally prominent exultation in carnival, magic, and excess (connoting the feminine) point to the dialogic nature of the text.

Amy Katz Kaminsky points out that Latin American testimonial writing has been noted for its nonliterariness, 'a no-nonsense approach to getting the facts straight' which gives it 'a kind of discursive manliness' (*29*, p. 52). Such qualities predominate in the final chapters of *La casa* where the style is often clipped and matter of fact, even unliterary in its insistence on direct communication: 'A los pocos meses se pudieron apreciar los resultados' (329), i.e. following economic sabotage by the Right; 'Así estaban las cosas cuando los camioneros se declararon en huelga' (330); 'El Presidente apareció en televisión pidiendo paciencia' (331). This mode of writing, though important, is only one among several modes of discourse deployed throughout a text whose departure from realist practice, and coincidence with certain postmodernist trends, are striking.

Allende's playful shuffling of various levels of reality (the magical and the mundane, the mythic and the historic, the irrational and the rational) both indicate her affinity with postmodernist writing and suggest her feminist interrogation of male structures of knowledge. Fantasy disturbs what has been taken to be real, tracing a space within society's cognitive frame.[30] This aspect of Allende's writing may appear at first sight to be at odds with her social preoccupations: the various styles represented in the text would seem to clash with serious reflection on the realities of the world, obscuring the clarity and force which the communication of social message demands. On the other hand, however, the instability of style and perspective has positive social implications. If no single reality exists, then no world view is definitively correct, no society can be deemed permanent or stable; and fantasy, representing flux and change, provides a telling counter-weight to the inexorable workings of destiny and historical process.

Magical Realism and Myth

When the setting of a text is conventional reality, the appearance of the fantastic has a dislocating effect, whether the reader eventually resolves the abnormal phenomenon on the side of the supernatural (since it indisputably contravenes natural laws), or on the side of the uncanny, where the abnormal phenomenon is finally resolved without recourse to the supernatural.[31] Magical realism produces such an effect by challenging the reader's habitual perceptions while at the same time refusing to locate the magical outside the realm of ordinary experience. The term 'magical realism' dates back to 1925 where it is found in the German title of a work by the art critic Franz

---

[30] This point is usefully discussed by Rosemary Jackson in *Fantasy: the Literature of Subversion* (London: Routledge, 1988), p. 23.

[31] I use here the distinctions offered by Tzvetan Todorov, *The Fantastic: A Structural Approach to a Literary Genre*, trans. by Richard Howard (Cleveland, OH: The Press of Case Western Reserve University, 1973), p. 41.

Roh: *Nachexpressionismus, magischer Realismus: Probleme der neuesten europäischen Malerei*. As Seymour Menton has pointed out, the term became known in Latin America through the 1927 *Revista de Occidente* translation of Roh's book (*33*, p. 9). Since then it has been used so widely and indiscriminately that some critics now question its usefulness — among them González Echevarría, who dismisses the term as 'un vacío teórico y a veces una nulidad histórica' (quoted in *8*, p. 23). For other critics, the term retains its validity: 'realismo mágico suple la necesidad de un término referente a lo que no entra en el dominio de lo irreal ni se confina enteramente en un orden natural y que alude tanto a motivos americanos como a otros de patrimonio universal'.[32] The reference here to 'patrimonio universal' is significant since some critics, such as Ángel Flores, have attempted — unsuccessfully — to claim magical realism as an exclusively Latin American literary phenomenon; others, notably Amaryll Chanady, have acknowledged its international status within the broader framework of avant-garde literature, while still claiming for it an original Latin American core deriving from 'creative "cannibalization"'.[33] Accepting the magical realist tag for her own work, Allende's view of this peculiar literary phenomenon follows Chanady rather than Flores (see *12*, p. 180 for her comments). As its name implies, magical realism reconciles concepts which are normally opposed, and inhabits the boundary between them.

---

[32] Lorraine Elena Ben-Ur, 'El realismo mágico en la crítica hispanoamericana', *Journal of Spanish Studies*, 4 (1976), 149–63 (p. 161).

[33] Amaryll Chanady, 'The Territorialization of the Imaginary in Latin America: Self Affirmation and Resistance to Metropolitan Paradigms in Magical Realism', in *31*, pp. 125–44, dismantles Ángel Flores's appropriation of magical realism as a Latin American phenomenon. See Ángel Flores, 'Magical Realism in Spanish American Fiction', *Hispania (USA)*, 38 (1955), 187–92. Noting the influence of surrealism on practitioners of magical realism such as Alejo Carpentier and Miguel Ángel Asturias, Chanady concludes that magical realism cannot be attributed to 'the supposed marvelous reality of the continent or ascribed to the unidirectional flow of metropolitan influence' (p. 141). Among the factors she identifies as having conditioned the phenomenon are 'a critical stance with respect to canonical rational and especially positivistic paradigms in the context of neocolonial resistance' (p. 141).

Chanady remarks that 'magical realism belongs neither entirely to the domain of fantasy (the creation of a world totally different from ours), nor to that of reality, our conventional everyday world' (*26*, p. 27). The supernatural often features prominently in magical realist texts (such as García Márquez's *Cien años de soledad*), offering a level of reality no less valid — and often all the more attractive — for being at odds with Western rational principles. An equally important strand of magical realist writing (such as Alejo Carpentier's *Los pasos perdidos*) does not resort to the supernatural, but rather focuses on the otherness of indigenous realities, or illuminates the marvellous side of familiar phenomena which have lost their wonder through long familiarity and the conditioning of an exclusively rational perspective. Grethe Jürgens's definition of magical realism focuses precisely on this aspect:

> It is the discovery of a whole new world. One paints pots and piles of rubbish and sees new things in a completely different way as if one had never before seen a pot. One paints a landscape, trees, houses, vehicles, and one sees the world anew. One discovers like a child a land of adventure. (quoted in *33*, p. 40).

A key feature of magical realism is authorial reticence: the ordinary is not differentiated from the marvellous and the supernatural is not presented as problematic. The reader is disconcerted not by the intrusion of the extraordinary into an otherwise normal world but rather by the blurring of boundaries between realities which he has been accustomed to keep apart. The frontiers between the real and unreal, truth and fiction, are broken down since there is no single reality or single truth. At the same time, the natural is contaminated by the supernatural, the banal by the marvellous and vice-versa. Such fusion of normally distinct realities informs the magical realism of Clara's childhood world 'donde se confundían la verdad prosaica de las cosas materiales con la verdad tumultuosa de los sueños [...]' (84). Thus the rather commonplace activity of embroidering a tablecloth is transformed, in Rosa's hands, into a surreal creation of 'bestias imposibles' (13) who belong to dream rather than to reality. The Latin American background is also significant here: Allende refers to 'un continente donde no hace falta inventar mucho, porque la realidad siempre nos sobrepasa' (*15*, p. 136).

In *La casa*, the magical intrudes not only into the fabric of daily life but, more surprisingly perhaps, into the political context, often with reinvigorating effect. In *Paula*, Allende states that the ghost of General Prats, the assassinated supporter of her uncle, Salvador Allende, returned to haunt Pinochet's wife and that Pinochet built a fortress to protect himself from 'enemigos vivos y muertos' (*1*, p. 248). It is however, the downside of magical realism, the fantastically ugly and grotesque, which is associated with the political barbarism portrayed in *La casa*. In the negative as well as the positive, the reality of Latin America outstrips the imagination.

One reason for the appeal of magical realism to Europeans is that it recalls their long-forgotten mythic past. The rise of rationalism resulted in what Marshall Berman terms a 'unity of disunity', cutting man off from his past, but it did not, of course, suppress entirely the powers of enchantment.[34] The Romantics, of course, rediscovered the emotional directness of personal experience and looked back with longing to the mythic past. More recently, postmodernism has promoted renewed interest in myth. The work of Karl Jung was crucial in this respect, given its focus on the myth-creating levels of the mind and its ready embrace of a supernatural level of reality. Whereas science atomizes, myth moves towards wholeness, a re-membering of the *homo totus* through a process of remembering.[35] Such purpose is central to Allende's own writing: 'Maybe the most important reason for writing is to prevent the erosion of time, so that memories will not be blown away by the wind' (*2*, pp. 44–45).[36]

---

[34] Marshall Berman, *All that is Solid Melts into Air: The Experience of Modernity* (London: Verso, 1983), p. 15.

[35] For a useful discussion on this point, see David Meakin, *Hermetic Fictions: Alchemy and Irony in the Novel* (Keele: Keele University Press, 1995), p. 80.

[36] Timothy Brennan claims that *La casa*, like Christa Wolf's *The Quest for Christa T*, 'is primarily a study of the recovery of memory through writing',

Myth goes back to the childhood of humanity. Despite the onslaught of rationalist currents, religious traditions remained vibrant even in secularized cultures — albeit in frequently diminished and distorted forms. In Latin America such pre-modern traits are more profoundly present, forming a network of shared meanings and a concrete social practice, and challenging the supremacy of official culture. In their study of Latin American popular culture, William Rowe and Vivian Shelling point out that 'the magic that continued to be practised by the lower orders of society became an alternative knowledge, from below. [...] It was a syncretism of native Indian, African and popular European belief, shared by different social classes, located in the interstices rather than the official structures of society, and was primarily the province of woman'.[37] The now stereotyped associations of the female with intuition and feeling can also be applied to myth which, unlike scientific thought, is not demonstrative or analytic, but narrative and fantastic, emotional and given to play rather than fixed in earnest pursuit of objectivity and truth (*37*, p. 29).

Though apparently clearcut, this difference requires some qualification in the light of the postmodernist realization that even scientific rationality, often seen as a largely male preserve, is ultimately a myth: the blurring of these gendered boundaries echoes the postmodernist disturbance of human gender divisions. The mythic revival attempts to articulate the 'unsaid' of rationalism, which had sought to establish a kind of mental dictatorship and banish the unreasonable other. The postmodern represents in this respect a feminization of culture as Christine Buci-Glucksman argues:

> In the labour of writing, the metaphor of the feminine
> then rises up as an element in the break with a certain
> discredited rationality based upon the idea of a historical

---

Salman Rushdie and the Third World: Myths of the Nation (London: Macmillan, 1989), p. 335.

[37] William Rowe and Vivian Schelling, *Memory and Modernity: Popular Culture in Latin America* (London: Verso, 1991), p. 214.

and symbolic continuum. It does this by designating a
new heterogeneity, a new otherness.[38]

If modernity is marked by instability, so is myth: on the one hand,
myth is comforting since it goes back to origins, seeking to fulfil the
desire to be at one with a cosmic beginning in a continual present, an
eternal now. Myth offers cyclical patterns that envelop both
characters and events, and it works by means of the archetype, an
original or founding image or figure. Myth therefore bears the
imprint of various kinds of repetition and thereby produces meaning;
it seems to offer stability, but is, in fact, dynamic and evolving,
despite its promise of closure. Myth needs the re-telling and re-
interpretation which modern literature has so richly provided, often
through irony.

Postmodernism welcomes myth both as a kind of antidote to
reason, and more importantly, as a figure of the heterogeneous
comings and goings of deregulated world views. Referring to
Nietzsche's and Heidegger's interpretation of instability at the level
of the individual, Vattimo maintains that 'they are trying to show us
how to take the experience of oscillation in the postmodern as an
opportunity to a new way of being (finally, perhaps) human' (37, p.
11). This returns us to Allende's brand of magical realism which is
ultimately concerned with the exploration of human potentialities in
a variety of spheres: historical, political, imaginary, magical, and
linguistic. For her, literature is not an end in itself but rather a
magical means of communication, which can weave together these
various strands; writing is politically charged but it is also performed
in a kind of trance and surpasses fact and reason.

Oscillation characterizes the reading experience of *La casa*, in
which the realist discourse of sociopolitical documentation merges
and clashes with those of popular custom, supernatural power, and
carnivalesque excess. These discourses enjoy equal validity in a text
which refuses hierarchical distinctions — as might be expected,
since the main narrator, Alba, constructs her narrative on the basis of

---

[38] Christine Buci-Glucksmann, *Baroque Reason: The Aesthetics of
Modernity*, trans. by Patrick Camiller (London: Sage, 1994), p. 49.

Clara's carnivalesque notebooks. From the outset, the reader is aware of a heterogeneous narrative world whose diverse elements just contrive to maintain a precarious balance:

> El día que llegó Barrabás era Jueves Santo. Venía en una jaula indigna, cubierto de sus propios excrementos y orines, con una mirada extraviada de preso miserable e indefenso, pero ya se adivinaba — por el porte real de su cabeza y el tamaño de su esqueleto — el gigante legendario que llegó a ser. (9)

Here the narrator combines the commonplace and the scatalogical, the sublime and the mythic, the past and the future, the realistic and the hyperbolic, offering readers a foretaste of the text's rich discursive levels, which will prevent them from settling into any specific mode of interpretation. Allende's purpose is to defamiliar-ize her narrative world, not only by shifting her focus among several modes of perception and stylistic practices, but also by illuminating those unexpected links between traditionally opposed conceptual orders, presenting thereby a textual reality which is both familiar and unfamiliar. The inconsistent treatment of the magical aspects of reality — which appear both positively and negatively — also cont-ribute to the readers' sense of uncertainty. Carnivalesque excess takes them beyond the familiar limits of their everyday world, while the cyclical patterns which inform the text point both to recognition and meaning, and to change and instability.

The Supernatural

The text is replete with the terminology of the supernatural, ranging from the religious and doctrinal inflections of Padre Restrepo who refers to the temptations of the devil (10) and to Clara's purported possession by the devil (15), to such flippant references as that used to describe Esteban's virility — 'bastaba tumbar a una muchacha en el potrero y quedaba preñada inmediatamente, era cosa del demonio' (69–70). A clear note of deflation informs the description of the statue of Saint Sebastian, whose wounds are 'milagrosamente frescas gracias al pincel del Padre Restrepo' (10). Elsewhere, references to the magical appear as mere figures of speech, which assume ironic overtones in the context of a magical realist text: thus, when Esteban prospers, 'sus negocios parecían tocados por una varilla mágica' (131) and, after the military coup, the shops are replenished with goods which 'parecían haber surgido como por obra de magia en las vitrinas' (353). The magical is distanced too when it is associated with the perspective of the primitive or of the child: cars are described as 'máquinas de fantasía' (71) and the magnet works by 'obra de magia' (135).

The supernatural is further distanced when its strangeness is foregrounded — an unusual procedure in La casa, and one generally confined to Esteban Trueba's narrative. The startling qualities of Rosa make Esteban 'estupefacto' and 'hipnotizado' (29) as his logical male mind, particularly given to classifying women and defining their roles (29, 70), is destabilized by Rosa's physical qualities which resist normal categorization: he refers to her 'increíble pelo verde' (29) and her 'belleza inhumana' (30). Elsewhere, the supernatural is occasionally distanced by rational explanation which obviously serves to deflate its power: 'La fantasía popular y la ignorancia respecto a su raza atribuyeron a Barrabás características mitológicas' (27).

Similarly, it is Clara's quixotic imagination, stimulated by the illustrations in the fantastic books of her uncle Marcos, that transforms Dr Cuevas, an 'hombronazo bonachón', into a 'vampiro gordo y oscuro' (44). The focalization of these instances deliberately portrays the supernatural and fantastic as categories alien to the rational mind. However, popular custom and superstitious practice are most often treated positively: when Marcos, Clara's uncle, reappears after his own funeral — he had been presumed dead after his flying mission — his survival is attributed to 'los rosarios clandestinos de las mujeres y los niños' (22). It is old Pedro García's mystical communion with the ants which succeeds in removing them from the estate rather than the technical expertise of the gringo Mr Brown. Even more impressive is the old peasant's success — which owes more to his invocation of the saints than to any medical training — in re-setting Esteban's bones crushed during the earthquake, a task which the supposed expert, Dr Cuevas, would not even have attempted (156).[39]

This oscillating perspective, which dismisses as well as vindicates magical practice, is most clearly seen at work at the end of Chapter 4 (135–37). First, the magical is presented from the point of view of the children, Blanca and Pedro, who enter a fantasy world clearly demarcated from reality since it is generated by Marcos's magic books. The distinction between fact and fiction blurs, however, when Pedro García displays to the children his very real talents in the mystical spheres of water-divining and herbal cures: there is further reference here to the superiority of his healing methods over those of orthodox medicine ('en ese terreno su sabiduría era tan grande, que el médico del hospital de las monjas iba a visitarlo para pedirle consejo'; 136). But then Pancha's death upsets the principle of unorthodox superiority, just as it seemed to be gaining firm foundation: not only do the old man's remedies fail, but they hasten the death of a patient who would have been cured by conventional practice. The chapter ends, however, with yet another change of perspective that restores narratorial vindication of Pedro García who now recounts to the children the political fable about the hens that united to subdue the predatory fox: Blanca's dismissive reaction exposes her crude, essentialist view of human nature, while Pedro's understanding of the tale's simple truth marks his coming of age. Allende queries traditional hierarchies but refuses to create new ones by simply inverting the old: the manifestations of the 'low other', represented here by Pedro García's popular remedies, are not permitted to consolidate and secure their frequent superiority over 'high' official practice.[40]

---

[39] While Pedro García's achievement arouses the incredulous admiration of the medical profession, the talents of the Romanian magician Rostipov who 'mejoraba la histeria con varillas magnéticas y trances hipnóticos' (76) in his spare time, causes outrage — perhaps, ironically, because these are seen as devilish rather than divine methods.

[40] Stalleybrass and White in *The Politics and Poetics of Transgression* (London: Methuen, 1986), pp. 178–81, use this terminology to define the

The treatment of the main characters' supernatural powers (particularly Clara's) is similarly ambiguous. Her powers range from making the salt cellar move by sheer psychic power (15) to predicting disasters such as her brother Luis's riding accident (16). Ignoring his sister's warning, Luis pays for his typical male disregard for the female realm of supernatural insight. Clara, for her part, does not appear to suffer any ill effects, following her publicly-expressed doubts about the existence of the devil (14), which perhaps confirms her belief in positive, rather than negative, spiritual energy. She also predicts the earthquake,[41] and interprets dreams (such as that of the gardener, Horacio, 78); she foresees the death of her mother Nívea in a dream (117). The efforts of other characters to predict the future are generally unsuccessful. One of the Mora sisters, Luisa, does predict correctly that Esteban's side will be victorious (346) but Férula's curse on Esteban — 'siempre estarás solo, se te encogerá el alma y el cuerpo y te morirás como un perro' (130) proves to be largely inaccurate. Though he feels abandoned by Clara and Blanca, Esteban forms a happy relationship with Alba and is attended both by her and by the spirit of Clara at his death. Whether he actually shrank physically or not remains uncertain: medical opinion dismisses the notion as fantasy (233) but Alba refers to photographic evidence which, she claims, proves that it happened (409). Even Clara herself is fallible: she 'forgets' to predict an earth tremor ('un temblor de tierra que Clara olvidó predecir', 211) and her intuitive powers fail to locate the young Blanca (104) and later Férula (130), and also to detect Nicolás's drug-taking (210). She herself is uncertain of the origins of the spiritual messages she receives, wondering whether they might come from beings from other planets rather than from the souls of the departed (201). Clara remains in spirit with her family after her death (Alba immediately goes to the

---

'base' languages of carnival (the festival of the Other) from which bourgeois society increasingly distanced itself.

[41] Jung attributed an inner upheaval within his own mind to some disturbance in the external world. Allende's treatment of the supernatural recalls Jung although there is no reason to infer direct influence, particularly in view of Allende's dismissive mockery of Jungian (and Lacanian) psychoanalysis (*1*, p. 315).

basement to await her grandmother's return; 279), and Luisa Mora brings a reassuring message to Alba from Clara, though she emphasizes that Clara's power to protect her is not limitless: 'los espíritus protectores son ineficaces en los cataclismos mayores' (346). The note of irony discernible here emerges more explicitly elsewhere: unlike his brother Nicolás, Jaime has no truck with spiritualism and in order to divert Amanda, who is about to undergo an abortion, he relates to her the story of the Spanish ghost that recently appeared to Clara 'con el cuento de que había un tesoro escondido en las fundaciones de la casa' (229). When the brothers take Amanda to their home, Clara asks no questions, unless — as the ironic narrator remarks — 'las hizo directamente a los naipes o los espíritus' (231–32). Clara's spiritual activities appear comic when she resorts to suspending a pendulum above the letters of the alphabet to induce extraterrestial messages delivered in Spanish and Esperanto. Subsequently, she makes eccentric and futile attempts to persuade successive Education Ministers of the importance of Esperanto. Further irony at Clara's expense emerges when she attributes — albeit in jest — the strange happenings reported by Blanca from her large house in the desert to 'el color del desierto, el embarazo y tu deseo inconfesado de vivir como una condesa' (238): despite her intimacy with the spirit world, Clara uses stereotyped common-sensical arguments to explain away real instances of black magic.

Irony of a bleaker kind informs the impingement of the magical on the sociopolitical sphere: Clara may have predicted the earthquake (153) — unlike the later earth tremor — but her magic is powerless to deal with its effects: 'de nada le sirvieron la mesa de tres patas o la capacidad de adivinar el porvenir en las hojas del té, frente a la urgencia de defender a los inquilinos de la peste y el desconcierto' (159). Far from resisting political terror, the magical becomes an intrinsic part of it: Alba is unable to calculate the length of her imprisonment because 'la soledad, la oscuridad y el miedo le trastornaron el tiempo y le dislocaron el espacio' (386). The magical effects of Tránsito's mirrors and lights recall Alba's torment: 'podían multiplicar el espacio [...] crear al infinito y suspender el tiempo'

(395). Military magic emits a sinister energy, marked by irresolvable contradiction, as it seeks to overturn the rules of geography: 'Acomodaron los mapas, porque no había ninguna razón para poner el norte arriba [...]' (363). Here the magical is perverted by male interference in a sphere which is properly female, as the scornful Esteban is keen to emphasize (133). Despite his fascination with the supernatural, Nicolás's ponderous, analytical approach and misplaced urge to 'desenmascar milagros' (181) ensure his failure — comically signalled by the nihilistic mysticism of his 'Instituto de Unión con la Nada' (283). In complete contrast, the purposeful and effective intervention of Clara's spirit saves Alba from a premature death at the hands of Esteban García by giving her a magical piece of inspiration: 'Clara trajo la idea salvadora de escribir con el pensamiento, sin lápiz ni papel [...]' (391). It is Clara's magic which sparks Alba's regeneration and her subsequent writing of the narrative; it is her kind of spiritual feminism which is finally vindicated — against the grain of previous ironic under-cutting and apparent inefficacy in the social sphere.

Mythical Origins

The magical lies at the origins of myth and religion, both informed by the cyclical patterns of death and regeneration. Clara's powers run counter to the most basic scientific principles but they purport to go back to origins and to draw on sources of inspiration long lost to the rational mind. Clara is keenly aware of the value of the past and the purpose of her writing is to enable Alba to 'rescatar las cosas del pasado' (411). The importance of origins is indicated in the text by repeated allusions to the Bible whose myths offer archetypal stories relating to critical stages in human history, such as Creation, Fall, and Deliverance. The first chapter of *La casa* is suffused with such references (which complement the equally pervasive presence of the magical): Padre Restrepo refers to temptation, the defilement of the flesh, the torment of the damned. The earliest ages of humanity are recalled by the description of Rosa as the most beautiful creature born 'desde los tiempos del pecado original' (12). After Clara's outburst in church, the family leaves, fearing that the priest might turn them into pillars of salt, the Old Testament punishment visited on Lot's wife (Genesis 19.26). Marcos dresses in a loincloth, convinced that 'así predicaba el Nazareno' (18) and Marcos contrives to imitate Christ by his 'heroica resurrección' (22). Plagues signal divine displeasure in Allende's world (just as they do in García Márquez's *Cien años de soledad*) — the typhus plague has the hallmarks of a 'castigo divino' (131), and Esteban, who seeks out Pancha in the cool of the evening (61), develops in old age 'un rostro triste de patriarca bíblico' (393). The initial reference to the Biblical name Barrabás is echoed in the final line of the text (9, 411).

Mythology, using worldly, human terms to express the divine, compensates for the contemporary loss of modes of thought vital for the flowering of the human spirit. The mythical dimension, privileging feeling rather than logic, is associated with the feminine. Jung regarded myths as messages from the unconscious and Clara's messages from the spirits can be interpreted in this light. Myth seeks to reaffirm the unity of the human with the natural world and Allende's presentation of her main female characters as green world archetypes is significant: Rosa's green hair is inherited by Alba and the greenness of both women is related to the sea: they share 'el color marítimo del cabello' (255). Clara herself is described as a 'planta salvaje' (80) and Amanda as 'frutal y sinuosa' (221). Myth can represent an idealistic return to wholeness, the search for a lost paradise, partially realized by Blanca and her non-patriarchal lover, Pedro, through their unrepressed sexuality. After a long separation, they feel a certain distance from each other, since childhood is now past. But paradise is regained: 'Volvieron a ser dos niños que corren, se abrazan y ríen [...]' (141), and the perfect idyll of their renewed romance ('Ella tenía el pelo lleno de hojas secas, que él quitó una por una') is heightened by the emergence of new life in the natural world (142).[42]

---

[42] The 'green-world' archetype is discussed by Annis Pratt, *Archetypal Patterns in Women's Fiction* (Bloomington: Indiana University Press, 1981), pp. 16–24. Allende has expressed her own strong affinity with the natural world, particularly her love of trees, in typically hyperbolic terms: she

The young Alba displays the innocence and wholeness of young humanity, which disturbs the sexually repressed Esteban García. His subsequent discharge of violent energy is facilitated by the military's horrific rule of terror. Fascism represents in part a return to primitive uncivilized roots. Jo Labanyi points out that the mythical appeal, on the one hand to classical order, and on the other to primal instinctual energies, is not as contradictory as it might seem, for both are attempts to return to what is seen as an original wholeness (*30,* p. 14). Resenting the advent of the new (Salvador Allende's democratically elected socialist government), Esteban Trueba is convinced that 'era necesario un período de dictadura para que el país volviera al redil del cual nunca debió haber salido' (365). When his expropriated estate is returned to him, he finds it in ruins; to restore his authority, as well as to satisfy his craving for vengeance, he launches an orgy of primitive and irrational violence in which workers' cottages are burnt and animals killed (365–66). Though Esteban is clearly capable of violent excesses his conscience remains sensitive and makes him feel remorse. His bastard grandson, Esteban García, might be seen, in Jungian terms, as the shadow who imitates Esteban Trueba's gestures and copies his voice from afar (182). Unlike his grandfather, however, Esteban García is unrestrained by conscience: he is the 'criatura hosca y malvada' (183) seen by Alba as 'la bestia que la acechaba en las sombras' (312) who will bring tragedy upon the family. He is a caricature of male law and phallic power, represented respectively by his profession as a policeman, and by his erect member, to which he draws Alba's attention: ' —¿ Sabes qué es eso? — preguntó roncamente. —Tu pene — respondió ella [...]' (272). Alba disconcerts Esteban García, shaming him rather than being shamed by him. It is his men who break into Esteban Trueba's house and direct their primitive violence against the artifacts of culture and civilization they find there, burning books and smashing classical records (384). Here again the grandson exaggerates the grandfather's sins since Trueba himself 'consideraba el arte como una forma de perder el

---

claims that the forest arouses in her an emotion that is 'más intensa que el más perfecto orgasmo o el más largo aplauso' (*1,* p. 48).

tiempo' (302). On the other hand Esteban Trueba represents foreign influence: he wants his new house to be built 'como los nuevos palacetes de Europa y Norteamericana', as removed as it possibly can be from the native style (94).

Against this background Esteban García can be seen as representing the violent return of repressed native instincts, the assertion of the Latin American Caliban against the foreign forces of civilization. Esteban García's incestuous rape of Alba suggests a mythic return to an age when humanity had not yet learned to control its instinctual drives. Esteban Trueba is both like and unlike Esteban García in this respect: he is guilty of rape but not of incest; despite his general crassness, Trueba is not ignorant of Freudian categories, indicating his awareness of the Oedipus Complex while reflecting on Blanca's indifference towards him (171); it is rather fitting that such a patriarchal figure should resort to one of the most obtrusive master-discourses of our time.

Returning to roots holds danger as well as the promise of wholeness. The military are well aware of the people's continuing dependence on ritual and magic, 'la necesidad del pueblo de tener sus propios símbolos y ritos'; popular craving for the magical too is a side of reality which Marxism fails to satisfy (362). The military aim to address such needs by means of their 'planes mesiánicos' (369) and their desire to go back to beginnings and remodel the world to their advantage leads them to overturn the rules of history and geography (362–63). On the other hand, Roland Barthes has identified as the negative aspect of myth its longevity and resistance to change, its assumption of fixed eternal values and its aura of naturalness.[43] This conservative side of myth — opposed by the main female characters — is found in *La casa* in the form of those patriarchal values which inform Esteban's world view, and condition the lives of the peasant women. Myth also perpetuates itself effortlessly through the perception of time as cyclical, and of the present as a repetition of patterns which have taken shape in the past and which allow for no, or very little, change in the future.

---

[43] Roland Barthes, *Mythologies*, trans. by Annette Lavers (London: Paladin, 1973), pp. 142–43.

Cyclical Time

The narrative world of *La casa* is structured by cyclic patterns which affect both characters and events, and the future, constantly anticipated, is shown to be conditioned by the past. Characters are linked by physical characteristics (the green hair of Rosa and Alba, for example) and by personal qualities (the creative talent of Rosa, Blanca, and Alba is expressed respectively in their tapestry, pottery, and painting; 167, 257). Violence, both personal and political, seems to generate recognizable patterns: Esteban Trueba burns the cottages of the *inquilinos*; his belongings are burnt by Esteban García's men. Trueba attacks Pedro Tercero with an axe, cutting off three of his fingers (198); García cuts off three of Alba's fingers (398). The violent kiss which Esteban García forces on Alba (311) anticipates his later violation and torture of her (384–87). Doña Ester's solitary and agonizing death (89) is duplicated by that of her daughter, Férula (146), while, in contrast, the much loved Pedro García and Clara pass almost imperceptibly from life into death (182, 276) and their funerals are described in almost identical terms: (Esteban) 'quería que todos recordaran ese entierro como un acontecimiento' (184); 'El funeral de Clara fue un acontecimiento' (279). Rosa's literal poisoning (33) finds a figurative analogue in Pancha's moral poisoning of Esteban García (182). On a more positive note, Esteban's lonely vigil at Rosa's grave (41) anticipates his night-long stay with Clara's body (277–78), while his dream at the 'Cristóbal Colón' in which he repeats Clara's name to the puzzlement of Tránsito Soto (301) looks forward to the moment of his death when he also utters Clara's name (409). Marcos's flying exploit is recalled by the equally eccentric attempt by his great-nephew forty years later, though with the crucial difference that Marcos's machine, which resembles a gigantic bird, takes to the air amid much public acclaim, whereas Nicolás's 'salchicha inflable' belongs to a less heroic age: initially conceived as a publicity stunt for a soft-drink company, it remains grounded owing to bureaucratic impediments (20–21; 218–19). Less obviously, the witchdoctor's healing of Tío Mateo, who falls victim to the evil eye in Brazil (as Nívea recounts to Clara; 81), looks forward to Pedro García's equally miraculous healing of Esteban Trueba (156). Esteban's energies are duplicated in his sons — though harnessed to different purposes: Jaime dedicates himself to caring for the poor (282) while Nicolás, as self-appointed 'defensor de la virtud de las doncellas de Las Tres Marías' (181), inverts his father's role as their violator. On the international level, Latin America appears to be safely remote from the European war: 'los vagones llenos de muertos eran un clamor lejano' (71); but Chile will repeat the experience with its own 'furgones llenos de cadáveres' (368).

It is worth noting that similar characters, themes and political messages appear in later Allende texts: woman as angel figure re-emerges in *De amor y de sombra* (1984) in the description of Irene's 'ignorancia angélica' (p. 113). In *Eva Luna* (1987), the intimacy of the mother–daughter bond recalls similar relations in *La casa*: Eva learns about the magical dimension of reality and the art of story-telling from her mother, Consuelo (pp. 27–28). Awareness that injustice is not a natural phenomenon but is, rather, socially constructed, motivates the guerrilla fighter, Huberto Naranjo (p. 181) who recalls both Pedro Tercero and Miguel of *La casa*, while the mystical ideas of Nicolás of the same text find fanatical expression in the figure of Charles Reeves of *El plan infinito*, who eventually descends into humiliating madness (p. 65). Padre Larraguibal of the same novel (p. 91) is a mirror image of Padre Restrepo of *La casa* while Gregory Reeves echoes the idea expressed in *La casa* that Marxism will not work in Latin America (pp. 106–07). In addition, Gregory's first-person narratives parallel Esteban Trueba's contributions to *La casa*.

Mythic, cyclical time emerges even more emphatically in *La casa* through the insistent and explicit anticipation of future events and the occasional recollection of the past. As narrators, both Alba and Esteban use similar verbal formulae, which punctuate the text and remind the reader that the future has, in a sense, already taken place: 'medio siglo después', 'muchos años más tarde', 'mucho tiempo después', 'con el tiempo', 'varios años más tarde'. A greater degree of precision, however, is appropriate to reflect the enormity of Alba's abduction which had been foretold by Luisa Mora: as

Esteban recollects, 'diez meses y once días más tarde recordaría la profecía de Luisa Mora cuando se llevaron a Alba en la noche, durante el toque de queda' (346). It is often the shadow of future joy or tragedy which colours the present: the first chapter anticipates the election, 'medio siglo después', of Salvador Allende (20), while the armed intrusion into Esteban Trueba's house is anticipated both in the first chapter by the phrase 'medio siglo más tarde' (24) and in the ninth by 'muchos años después' (259–60). Family conflict is anticipated when Blanca and Pedro become childhood friends (104–05) while, on a more positive note, the family's final salvation is anticipated by Esteban Trueba's reference to Tránsito Soto's intervention 'mucho tiempo después' (117). This web of anticipation is reinforced both by some less obtrusive references to the future — Esteban's remark that it would take an earthquake to destroy his furniture (57) — and by explicit allusions to the forces of destiny: Esteban García, for example, 'estaba destinado a cumplir un terrible papel en la historia de la familia' (137). His subsequent description as the instrument of tragedy (183) points to human impotence rather than to freedom of action, as does the persistent emphasis on the characters' ignorance of the future: when Amanda promises to give her life for her little brother, Miguelito, the narrator comments: 'no sabía que algún día tendría que hacerlo' (213). (Amanda dies without betraying her brother; 404.) Conversely, the past is occasionally seen from the perspective of future events which confirm what had been foreseen: Blanca's pottery business flourishes in Canada, thereby fulfilling the prediction made by her former husband, Jean de Satigny, twenty-five years before (379). Human affairs are seemingly locked into a predetermined pattern, and history appears to preclude independent human action, being no more than 'una cadena de hechos que debían cumplirse' (410).

The Carnivalesque

The carnivalesque can be seen as a mode of release for those primitive energies — associated with the mythic past — that have been repressed by civilization. Informed by excess and exaggeration, it revels in transgressing rational and legal norms in its pursuit of the ludic and vulgar.[44] Emir Rodríguez Monegal has noted its peculiar importance in Latin America, relating it to the often brutal assimilation of foreign cultures, and the shock of imposed social structures such as Christianity and feudalism (*34*, pp. 407–08).

Carnival embodies the challenge of the low to official restraint and reason. Its underlying structural features operate beyond the strict confines of popular festivity. The carnivalesque mediates between, on the one hand, correctness and propriety — the standards to be followed — and, on the other, the improper and base, whose downward force is to be resisted. Like myth, carnival is anathema to bourgeois society which has often defined itself through its suppression of the base languages of carnival. But carnival, as Stalleybrass and White comment, continued to produce its ritual inversions: 'it links the inversion of hierarchy [...] with a comic privileging of the bottom part of the body [...] over the rational and spiritual control of the head' (Stalleybrass and White, p. 183).

Revelling in her reputation as a natural storyteller, Allende has acknowledged few specific sources of literary influence on her writing: 'Nunca pienso que estoy escribiendo una gran obra literaria, sino que una historia que le importa al lector. Soy una cuentacuentos [...]' (*12*, p. 107). Unsurprisingly, inspiration for this kind of talent comes from a rather unorthodox source, a collection of tales, the *Thousand and One Nights*:

> En esas páginas de amor, la vida y la muerte tenían un carácter juguetón; las descripciones de comida, paisajes, palacios, mercados, olores, sabores y texturas eran de tal riqueza, que para mí el mundo nunca volvió a ser el mismo. (*1*, p. 84)

---

[44] The carnivalesque functions as a figure of subversion in literature despite the dependence of carnival itself on social sanction which, as Eagleton points out, makes it a tame and circumscribed affair rather than a potent sign of defiance and ridicule. See Terry Eagleton's *Walter Benjamin: Or, Towards a Revolutionary Criticism* (London: Verso, 1981), p. 148.

Such carnivalesque spirit suffuses *La casa* which contains frequent references to extravagant festivities such as Blanca's wedding to Jean de Satigny, described as a 'fiesta caligulesca' with five hundred guests invading the *gran casa de la esquina* (205). Carnivalesque banqueting and drinking form an important part of the wedding and recall similar gastronomic opulence on the occasion of Esteban's engagement to Clara (91). Public spectacles also feature prominently: Marcos's flying exploit turns into a popular occasion: 'Hubo gente que viajó de provincia para ver el espectáculo' (20) while Nicolás's 'salchicha gigantesca rellena de aire caliente' (20) might have some Rabelaisian overtones given the later description of the engagement party of Esteban and Clara as 'un banquete pantagruélico' (91). (Rabelais's Pantagruel was a giant who encountered a flying pig.)

One essential element in carnival is, of course, laughter which is always directed at officialdom or authority: in *La casa*, Severo fears that Clara's outburst in church might provoke 'la risa colectiva' (14). Clara's displays of supernatural power are often subversively humorous, upsetting the staid, hierarchical routines of the household: 'algunas veces, a la hora de la comida, cuando estaban todos reunidos en el gran comedor de la casa, sentados en estricto orden de dignidad y gobierno, el salero comenzaba a vibrar y de pronto se desplazaba por la mesa entre las copas y platos [...]' (15). Clara's uncle, Marcos, may be seen as the low Other of her respectable father, the lawyer and aspiring politician, Severo del Valle. Marcos, like Clara, upsets the family's decorum and order, 'provocando el regocijo de los sobrinos, especialmente de Clara, y una tormenta en la que el orden doméstico perdía su horizonte' (17). Severo is only too aware of Marcos's impropriety: 'los modales del tío Marcos eran los de un caníbal, como decía Severo' (17). Marcos becomes a public spectacle and source of general amusement when he takes to serenading his cousin, Antonieta, to the accompaniment of a dilapidated barrel-organ and a screeching parrot uttering a language which itself fits the category of the low Other, being Amazonian in origin (17–18). The crowds are drawn by 'el placer de comprobar que también en las mejores familias había buenas razones para avergonzarse' (19). The housekeeper, La Nana, representing domestic authority and order, seeks to suppress the carnivalesque behaviour of both the parrot, whose 'mirada lujuriosa' and 'gritos destemplados' (19) she cannot tolerate, and of the dog, Barrabás, whose appearance alone draws public curiosity since his form appears to contradict the laws of the animal world: 'la gente lo creía una cruza de perro con yegua' (27). La Nana succeeds in eliminating the parrot with an overdose of codliver oil, but the same treatment fails to achieve the desired effect on Barrabás, causing merely a 'cagantina de cuatro días' which La Nana, bowing, one might say, to a carnivalesque code of justice, has to clean up herself (27).

Carnivalesque play in the text is also facilitated by various references to masks. The mask is associated with the most ancient rituals and spectacles: Clara finds that Férula has attempted to overcome the solitude of her last days by recourse to a motley collection of costumes and wigs, now jumbled chaotically together: 'todo revuelto en una hermandad grotesca' (146). Férula had attempted to escape her identity as a solitary spinster by assuming other roles, including those of admirals and bishops, in her attempt to become the man she had always wanted to be (50). In contrast, Tránsito Soto disguises herself as Aphrodite, 'con tres pisos de crespos en la cabeza, mal cubierta por unos tules drapeados y chorreando uvas artificiales desde el hombro hasta las rodillas', giving her 'un definitivo aspecto mitológico' (299). Masks are effective because they stimulate the erotic fantasies of the clients (299–300); the association with myth suggests a return to pre-oedipal urges, free of cultural constraints.

Unrestrained sexuality is a further aspect of carnivalesque excess: Esteban Trueba's sexual desires become all-consuming and extend beyond normal boundaries: 'comenzó a mirar con ojos de concupiscencia a las aves del corral, a los niños que jugaban desnudos en el huerto y hasta a la masa cruda del pan [...]' (60). Later, his prodigious powers of procreation (67) are matched by his equally prodigious ability to generate wealth (216, 378). Such loosening of sexual restraints impinges on the integrity of gender distinctions (Esteban is attracted by Tránsito's virility, 117; Nicolás

is described as 'hermoso como una doncella', 180), and gives rise to
illicit desires (Férula's love for Clara, 124, and Jaime's for his niece,
Alba, 335). Scatology, a further carnivalesque feature, informs much
of the text's humour and its obsession with low bodily functions: at
the first party held at *Las Tres Marías*, on the occasion of Esteban's
birthday, Férula is disturbed while using the toilet by the drunken
mayor who enters the room unbuttoning his flies and, instead of
withdrawing immediately, proceeds to introduce himself to Férula
(108). Pedro García's remedies involve the use of cow and horse
dung, but fail to cure Pancha's 'diarrea interminable' (136). Clara,
however, is the outstanding representative of the carnivalesque spirit,
combining her celestial aura ('un ser angélico y hermoso', 84) with
her 'despreocupada e impúdica sensualidad' (97). For Bakhtin,
'eccentricity is a special category of the carnival sense of the world
[...] it permits — in concretely sensuous form — the latent sides of
human nature to reveal and express themselves'. The carnival sense
of the world implies a weakening of seriousness and rationality:
Clara's response to Esteban's fury, when he discovers that she has
been attempting to raise feminist consciousness among the estate's
peasant women, is to ask him if he can wiggle his ears (106), perhaps
expressing here an unconscious affinity with what Bakhtin calls 'the
joyful relativity of everything'.[45] Clara's carnivalesque character is
also evident both in her madness (her 'quehaceres lunáticos', 111,
and her 'trances lunáticos', 164) which allows her to see with
different eyes, undimmed by the normal, and in her 'desbordante
imaginación' shared by all the women in her family (11).

Clara's anarchic imagination is often contrasted with Esteban's
patriarchal sense of order: the clash between them emerges starkly in
their distinct architectural tastes: Esteban favours classical order and
precision with ostentatious grounds boasting fountains and statues of
Greek gods. Clara upsets the symmetry of *la gran casa de la esquina*
on the one hand by constructing architectural supplements in the
form of 'protuberancias y adherencias, de múltiples escaleras

---

[45] Mikhail Bakhtin, *Problems of Dostoevsky's Poetics*, trans. and ed. by
Caryl Emerson, Theory and History of Literature, 8 (Minneapolis:
University of Minnesota Press, 1984), pp. 123, 125.

torcidas que conducían a lugares vagos [...]' (94) and, on the other, by knocking down walls in search of hidden treasure or unburied bodies mentioned to her by the spirits, with the result that Esteban's once decorous residence is converted into 'un laberinto encantado imposible de limpiar, que desafiaba numerosas leyes urbanísticas y municipales' (95). These styles correspond to Carpentier's distinction between the classical, which is imitative and unoriginal, the architectural expression of tyranny and petrification, and the baroque which rejects symmetry in favour of 'desmesura', inordinate dimensions, and goes back to America's origins: 'América, continente de simbiosis, de mutaciones, de vibraciones, de mestizajes, fue barroco desde siempre'.[46] Rosa's imagination is equally destructive of convention and logic, for her tapestry boasts creatures that are half bird and half mammal, 'tan gordas y con alas tan breves que desafiaban las leyes de la biología y de la aerodinámica' (13). Blanca, for her part, reinvents the magical tales recounted in Marcos's books, inverting in the process the familiar narrative archetypes of the fairy tale: 'Así se enteró Alba [...] de un lobo perdido en el bosque a quien una niña destripó sin razón alguna [...]' (288).

One curious episode in the text serves to highlight the procedures whereby high Western artistic authority seeks to co-opt and classify an art work representing an alien, low culture. Clara's portrait was painted by an impoverished artist who subsequently achieved fame. Sold by Alba to the British consul (378), it was subsequently placed in a London museum. Rejecting the expert view that the portrait bears the imprint of the Russian-born artist, Marc Chagall (1887–1985), Alba discounts the mediation of artistic conventions and claims that the portrait represents a perfect mirror of its subject: 'corresponde exactamente a la realidad que el artista vivió en la casa de Clara [...]' (254). This episode points to Western (male) incomprehension of a carnivalesque (female) Latin American reality which subverts 'las leyes de la física y la lógica' (254). The authorities respond by invoking artistic convention to classify and

---

[46] Alejo Carpentier, 'Lo barroco y lo real maravilloso', in *Ensayos: tientos y diferencias* (Havana: Letras Cubanas, 1984), pp. 108–26 (p. 116).

explain an art work expressive of the intuitive, the mythical and the supernatural. The rule of the high rational norm cannot be undermined by the challenge of the low primitive.

The very diverse images of the female body, found throughout the text, would seem to underlie the association of the female body with the carnivalesque. Indeed the whole text might be seen as a celebration of the female form ranging from the blossoming adolescent body, by way of the socially conditioned and decrepit body, to the decaying and dead body. The monstrosity of Blanca's inchoate body (101) develops into uncontainable beauty (139). The angelic body of Rosa occupying in life 'un límite impreciso entre la criatura humana y el ser mitológico' (12) is finally reduced in death to 'un polvillo tenue y gris' (290). Esteban's perception of the grotesque aspect of the pregnant Pancha ('un enorme envase que contenía una substancia informe y gelatinosa'; 66) is matched by Miguel's perception of Alba's birth: 'la visión del gigantesco globo atravesado de venas y coronado por un ombligo sobresaliente, de donde salió aquel ser amoratado, envuelto en una horrenda tripa azul' (251). The erotic body of Tránsito Soto (300) seems to have nothing in common with the withered bodies of the peasant women at *Las Tres Marías* 'con sus bocas desdentadas y sus ojos llenos de arrugas, curtidas por el sol y la mala vida' (106), but both are socially constructed. Alba's tortured body experiences in this world (386–87) the torments which Padre Restrepo had promised for the next: 'las carnes desgarradas por ingeniosas máquinas de tortura' (10), while the depraved contrivances at Tránsito's brothel ('potros de tormento'; 395) produce a carnivalesque conjunction of perverse sexual gratification and torture taken to the limit. The grotesque is also represented by the decaying body of doña Ester (88) and the dead body of Férula (147).

The female body is frequently mutilated in circumstances redolent of carnival: Rosa's autopsy takes place not in a hospital but on a dining room table, with a salad bowl to hold her intestines (44); Nívea's head, severed from her body in a car accident, is not placed in a coffin but stored in a hat box (122), until it is finally buried with Clara (279). Carnival infects the tragic with the comic and vice-versa, promoting a kind of Bakhtinian relativity, and destabilizing, to a certain extent, the apparently documentary seriousness of the final chapters. These bodies which form a kaleidoscopic series of shifting images, moving from pleasure to pain, from vitality and promise to decline and decay, contribute to the carnivalesque aspect of the text which is marked by instability and change rather than fixity and order. This difference is encapsulated in the contrast between Salvador Allende, associated by his opponents with the spirit of carnival ('circulaban fotografías burdamente trucadas que lo mostraban vestido de Baco'; 362) and the image of Augusto Pinochet whose vanity is subjected to carnivalesque deflation by the reference to the Cuatro Espadas monument whose eternal torch emits not a flame but kitchen smoke, and by the punning allusion to his 'augustos bigotes' (357).

Parody, in Bakhtin's definition, is inseparably linked to a carnival sense of the world (*Problems of Dostoievsky's Poetics*, p. 127). *La casa* sometimes appears to indulge in self-parody through its relentless exaggerations: the absurdity of a dog's tail reaching the length of a golf club (26), and the bathos of Rosa's angelic beauty causing traffic jams (29), alert the reader to the comic spirit of the text. The characters themselves are deliberately depicted as larger than life, given to extreme emotions and passions, personifying extreme virtues, or extreme vices. The description of Férula is conspicuous not so much for what it communicates about her as for its linguistic excess:

> Era uno de esos seres nacidos para la grandeza de un solo amor, para el odio exagerado, para la venganza apocalíptica y para el heroísmo más sublime, pero no pudo realizar su destino a la medida de su romántica vocación, y éste transcurrió chato y gris [...]. (108)

Though often overwhelming, Esteban's anger and pride fall short of the intensity of his 'amor desmedido' for Clara (127), though the hatred he and Férula nurture for each other grows 'hasta que ocupó toda la casa' (128). Clara's extremes of eccentricity and self-absorption make her oblivious to the stunning physical changes in her daughter Alba (139). Jaime and Nicolás are very different characters but are equally given to extravagant behaviour: banished from his father's house, Nicolás takes revenge by undressing outside the Congress building where his father is a Conservative senator (284). Jaime is just as eccentric — 'desde niño tenía gestos extravagantes' (179) — but he directs his energies towards helping others, though his efforts are so extreme that he too succeeds in embarrassing his father: having removed his trousers, which he gives to a pauper, he is followed home by 'una leva de niños y curiosos que lo vitoreaban' (218). This unlikely situation is surpassed by the colourful background of Blanca's Jewish suitor who found prosperity and fame as the 'Rey de las Ollas a Presión' after surviving a concentration camp (263). Love-making assumes an exaggerated intensity and original freshness for Blanca and Pedro (152) and for Alba and Miguel whose love at first sight (303) is followed by overwhelming passion: 'se amaron con desespero hasta que sintieron que se les escapaba la vida y les reventaba el alma [...]' (374). Textual extravagance and ostentation are not toned down in the final chapters where the focus remains on the limits of human love, endurance, sacrifice, and hatred. The President, in his radio broadcast, makes the heroic promise to sacrifice his life (349), and Jaime's subsequent refusal to confirm the lie that Allende committed suicide suggests the limits of human courage: 'Haga esa declaración usted mismo. Conmigo no cuenten, cabrones' (351). Amid the violence and horror of the conclusion, the spirit of carnival survives. A kind of carnivalesquely perverse dethronement underlies the funeral ('ese modesto desfile'; 368) of the great Nobel Prize-winning poet Pablo Neruda who is buried in a borrowed grave. Alba, nicknamed 'condesa' by her teacher, Sebastián Gómez, after he noticed her being chauffeur-driven to university (307), resigns herself to an existence of filth and squalor in prison: 'se resignó a su propia inmundicia y dejó de pensar en la insoportable necesidad de lavarse' (386). The world is truly turned upside down: words cannot be used as they were before (383); Alba's sensual pleasure (383–84) gives way to sensual suffering (385) and everyday points of reference to time and space are overturned (386). Ironically, the gentle morning light hurts the eyes of Alba whose name means 'dawn' (389). The more comic spirit of carnival re-emerges explicitly in the final reference to Esteban's physical shrinking which had appeared ambiguous, sometimes presented as factual, sometimes as the figment of Esteban's imagination (175, 233, 278, 290, 395). Alba seems to resolve the issue by reference to photographic evidence, which confirms that her grandfather had actually got smaller (409). Esteban's carnivalesque metamorphosis into the dwarf of his former self offers a low physical analogue of the diminution of his high spiritual being.

The diverse aspects of *La casa* discussed here remove the text from the narrow limits of historical writing. The magical realist, mythic, and carnivalesque elements give rise to sustained ambiguity and destabilize the reading experience, pointing to *La casa*'s close affinities with postmodernist literature. If there is any stability here it is to be found in the general alignment of the masculine with fixity, reaction, and predictability and the feminine with change, vitality, and excess.

5. Technique and Style

According to Aníbal González, documentary narratives deal with fundamental polar oppositions: truth versus falsehood, justice versus injustice, society versus the individual (*28*, p. 124). As a documentary novel, *La casa* conforms in some respects to this neat definition: Allende the testimonial writer trades in such simple distinctions and her language is often plainly referential, the magic of words overshadowed by their functional purpose of recording historical reality. However, it is the postmodern and hybrid quality of the text which leaves the more lasting impression. In documenting the painful past, the novel belongs to the most searingly trenchant strand of resistance writing, dedicated to the disclosure of suppressed, 'unofficial' history,[47] but this aspect is matched by the wholly literary impulse of the ludic and frivolous. Allende's language refers to the reality of pain and torture but it also freewheels in suggestive self-referential mode, signifying not so much the world outside the text as the author's indulgence in linguistic play. In an essay entitled 'La magia de las palabras', Allende discusses her passion for words, which enable her to relate the truth about her country but, in addition, allow her to indulge in a kind of unregulated carnivalesque discourse: 'infinitas palabras para combinarlas a mi antojo, para burlarme de ellas o tratarlas con respeto, para usarlas mil veces sin temor a desgastarlas' (*3*, p. 448).

The testimonial aspect of the text is evident and has been noted by several critics: Riquelme Rojas and Edna Aguirre Rehbein, for example, claim that Allende's personal experience 'allows her to transmit firsthand the historical development of the continent' (*13*, p. 3) and Teresa Huerta notes with reference to both *La casa* and *De*

---

[47] For a thoroughgoing and perceptive discussion of such writing, see Barbara Harlow, *Resistance Literature* (London: Methuen, 1987).

amor y de sombra that Allende 'crea una novela de tipo testimonio' (*16*, p. 56). Testimony implies a subject as witness to and participant in public events; one of the best definitions is provided by George Yúdice:

> una narración auténtica, contada por un *testigo* quien está movido hacia el *narratorio* por la *urgencia* de la situación (por ejemplo: guerra, opresión, revolución, etc). Con énfasis sobre el *discurso oral popular*, el testigo retrata su propia *experiencia* como *representativa* de una *memoria e identidad colectivas*. *La verdad* está invocada con el objetivo de *denunciar* la situación de explotación y opresión o *exorcisar* y *corregir* la historia oficial. (*36*, p. 85)

Allende has consistently emphasized the political purpose of her work: 'siento que soy [...] una voz que habla por los que sufren y callan' (*12*, p. 106). Testimonial writing is driven by the determination to challenge official versions of events and in *La casa* 'la versión oficial' relating to President Allende's death is exposed as lacking any credibility (354). The most explicit reference to *testimonio* within the text is to be found in the final chapter, when Clara's spirit infuses the imprisoned Alba with new life and purpose: 'le sugirió, además, que escribiera un testimonio, que algún día podría servir para sacar a la luz el terrible secreto que estaba viviendo [...]' (391). It is significant here that *testimonio*, often rooted in the 'práctica de lo cotidiano' and peopled by 'héroes de la banalidad' (*36*, p. 109), is inspired in *La casa* by a supernatural event. Alba proceeds to write a social history of twentieth-century Chile, culminating in the 1973 coup, based largely on three manuscript sources: the writings of her grandfather, Esteban, who contributed 'varias páginas' (409), the notebooks of her grandmother, Clara, and the letters of her mother Blanca (410).

References to the notebooks are found in most chapters and serve to reinforce and legitimize the text's documentary purpose. They highlight Clara's obsessiveness, her determination to preserve

events from the ravages of forgetfulness (78) and her painstaking
methodology: 'Clara describió esta escena con minuciosidad en su
diario, detallando con cuidado las dos habitaciones oscuras [...]'
(146). Such references also serve, however, to draw the reader's
attention to the way in which the text has been constructed, to its
self-consciousness. They have a dual effect, therefore, seeking to
reinforce the historical truth of the narrative, which is a constant
preoccupation of Alba — 'Todos los que vivieron aquel momento
coinciden en que eran alrededor de las ocho de la noche [...]'
(143) — but they also point to the mediation of writing. In addition
the distinct narrative perspectives of Alba and Esteban point to
artistic manipulation rather than plain documentation. Alba is
identified as the main narrator only in the epilogue and previous
first-person references (e.g. 9, 282) can be recognized only in
retrospect.

Reinforcing the testimonial character of the text is its
emphatically oral style: the peculiar power of the oral message is
highlighted through Pedro Segundo García's belief that his son
'había conseguido más adeptos con sus baladas subversivas que con
los panfletos del Partido Socialista [...]' (169). Esteban's style, often
colloquial and vulgar — 'me había puesto viejo, carajo' (175) —
assumes an oral, conversational quality when he shifts from the past
of the narrated events to the present of his writing: 'por eso no puedo
aceptar que mi nieta me venga con el cuento de la lucha de clases,
porque si vamos al grano, esos pobres campesinos están mucho peor
ahora que hace cincuenta años' (56–57). Alba's style is similarly
marked by the directness of oral speech and she too resorts
occasionally to vulgar expression (Barrabás's 'cagantina', 27;
Jaime's 'pantalones tibios de mierda', 350). Like Esteban's, her
narrative switches rather abruptly from past to present: 'es una
delicia, para mí, leer los cuadernos de esa época [...]' (84); 'tengo un
retrato de Férula tomado en esos años [...]' (109). But the
conversational intimacy of such references is complemented by their
self-reflexiveness, with the sharper focus falling on the act of writing
in the present time of the narrator rather than on the events narrated.

Once more testimonial spontaneity and orality are qualified by introspective textual self-consciousness.

Allende's use of free indirect speech heightens the oral quality of the text. Rendered immobile by injuries sustained during the earthquake, Esteban is consumed by anger and frustration and his own words intrude into the third-person narrative in order to convey his feelings more directly: 'él se puso cada día más furibundo y despótico, le exigía ponme una almohada aquí, tengo hambre, tengo calor, ráscame la espalda, más abajo' (159). The same technique is used earlier to convey Férula's agitation following her confession to the priest — with abrupt transitions from the first-person commands she directs at the servants to the third-person narrative which confirms that her instructions have been carried out: '[...] exigiendo póngame esto aquí, se lo ponían, cambien las flores de los jarrones, las cambiaban [...]' (101).

Here the expressive elements of spoken speech are highlighted but so is artistic virtuosity since the reader has to make sense of the sudden and unannounced shifts of narrative perspective. Another technique which achieves a comparable effect is prolepsis, the anticipation of future events: the repeated use of such phrases as 'muchos años después' (259–60) suggests the suspense-creating procedures of oral story-telling but it also has the effect of increasing interest in the narrator and in her authorial manipulation of events. Alba's style inclines towards orality in other respects, notably through her breathless accumulation of verbs and nouns as in the description of the frantic love-making of Blanca and Pedro Tercero:

> [...] se besaron por todos lados, se lamieron, se mordieron, se chuparon, sollozaron y bebieron las lágrimas de los dos, se juraron eternamente y se pusieron de acuerdo en un código secreto que les serviría para comunicarse durante los meses de separación. (143)

This frenzied activity finds its stylistic counterpart in the excess of verbal energy which overwhelms the reader. Similarly the

accumulation of nouns cannot fail to impress in the following
description of Férula's costumes:

> De unos clavos en los muros colgaban trajes anticuados,
> boas de plumas, escuálidos pedazos de piel, collares de
> piedras falsas, sombreros que habían dejado de usarse
> hacía medio siglo, enaguas desteñidas con sus encajes
> raídos, vestidos que fueron ostentosos y cuyo brillo ya
> no existía, inexplicables chaquetas de almirantes y
> casullas de obispos, todo revuelto en una hermandad
> grotesca [...]. (146)

This emphatic listing gives the impression of lightness, of the chaotic
flow of unedited, spontaneous speech but it also, paradoxically,
creates an opposing sense of weight and solidity, of compression —
as if there were not enough time and space for everything to be said,
as if language were running out of steam leaving an unwritten
hinterland of suggested presence. Such listing also serves to disorient
the reader through its cumulative excess which foregrounds the play
of language and blurs meaning. Elsewhere the breathless rhythm of
long sentences complements their meaning: repetition and free
indirect speech in the following passage suggest relentlessness and
immediacy and reinforce the reader's sense of the frenetic pace of
urban life which alarms the countrified Esteban:

> La ciudad le pareció desconocida, había un desorden de
> modernismo, un prodigio de mujeres mostrando las
> pantorrillas, de hombres con chaleco y pantalones con
> pliegues, un estropicio de obreros haciendo hoyos en el
> pavimento, quitando árboles para poner postes, quitando
> postes para poner edificios, quitando edificios para
> plantar árboles, un estorbo de pregoneros ambulantes
> gritando las maravillas del alfilador de cuchillos, del
> maní tostado, del muñiquito que baila solo, sin alambre,
> sin hilos, compruébelo usted mismo, pásele la mano, un
> viento de basurales, de fritangas, de fábricas, de

> automóviles tropezando con los coches y los tranvías de
> tracción a sangre, como llamaban a los caballos viejos
> que tiraban la movilización colectiva, un resuello de
> muchedumbre, un rumor de carreras, de ir y venir con
> prisa, de impaciencia y horario fijo. Esteban se sintió
> oprimido. (85)

This extract also illustrates a related stylistic peculiarity, prominent
throughout the text: a seemingly interminable sentence capped by a
short summary statement as if the speaker is pausing to draw breath.
Enumeration, a hallmark of Allende's style, often takes the form of
three lexical units. This characteristic and conspicuous feature
— often concentrated in short textual segments — gives Allende's
prose an insistent, jingling rhythm, suggestive of an experienced
storyteller who knows his tale so well that he can fine-tune its oral
impact. On arriving at his run-down estate, 'Las Tres Marías', the
disgusted Esteban 'dio orden de guardar al niño, lavar el patio y
matar al perro' (56); shortly afterwards the frustrated Esteban 'se
dejaba flotar a la deriva, sintiéndose abrazado por la corriente,
besado por los guarisapos, fustigado por las cañas de la orilla' (60).
Sometimes such parallel structures are used to produce an erotic
effect: Jaime and Nicolás are initiated sexually by a 'mujerona
inmensa que podía acunarlos a los dos en sus pechos de vaca
holandesa, ahogarlos a los dos en la pulposa humedad de sus axilas,
aplastarlos a los dos con sus muslos de elefante y elevarlos a los dos
a la gloria con la cavidad oscura, jugosa, caliente, de su sexo' (126).
Both the insistent alliteration and the rhythm enhance the sense of
voluptuous sexuality which assumes carnivalesque proportions.
Elsewhere the same techniques are used to different purpose,
suggesting the fleeting pubescence, vulnerability, and imminent
violation of Pancha: 'la había observado cuando lavaba la ropa,
agachada en las piedras planas del río, con sus piernas morenas
pulidas por el agua, refregando los trapos descoloridos con sus toscas
manos de campesina' (61). Here the slow and measured rhythm is
ominous, suggesting a lull before the storm of Esteban's assault.

In complete contrast with this lively intensity of style is the matter-of-fact documentation to be found at the end of the text: 'en los meses siguientes la situación empeoró mucho, aquello parecía un país en guerra. Los ánimos estaban exaltados especialmente entre las mujeres de la oposición, que desfilaban por las calles aporreando sus cacerolas en protesta por el desabastecimiento' (343). Here the intention is not to achieve poetic effects but rather to convey information with journalistic directness. To heighten the impact of the often poignant narrative Allende often resorts to short bursts of staccato sentences — to convey, for example, the torture of Jaime: 'lo sujetaron de los brazos. El primer golpe le cayó en el estómago. Después lo levantaron, lo aplastaron sobre una mesa y sintió que le quitaban la ropa. Mucho después lo sacaron inconsciente del Ministerio de Defensa' (351).

The most striking feature of Allende's style is its diversity: it ranges from the leisurely and descriptive (e.g. Esteban's visit to the luxurious Hotel Francés where he treats himself to tea; 48–49) to the hurried and curtly ominous ('el cielo comenzó a nublarse. Se oían algunos disparos aislados y lejanos'; 349); from the poetic ('la luna se reflejaba en el agua con un brillo de cristal y la brisa mecía suavemente las cañas y las copas de los árboles'; 190) to the colloquial and vulgar such as in the reference to Sofía of the Farolita Roja who was still able to 'impedir que se metieran los gendarmes a fregar la paciencia y a los patrones a propasarse con las muchachas, jodiendo sin pagar' (72). Transitions between styles are often abrupt: Alba's expansive hyperbolic and magical realist description of Barrabás, for example, giving way to Esteban's dour matter-of-fact narration — 'eran tiempos difíciles. Yo tenía entonces alrededor de veinticinco años […]' (27).

It is therefore its chaotic range of style and theme which distinguishes *La casa* rather than the often uniform and univocal discourse associated with testimonial writing — which is usually 'metodológicamente callado' (*36*, p. 120), unlike Allende's frequently self-conscious text. The testimonial style plays an important part in *La casa* and emerges forcefully in the text's obsession with historical accuracy and self-legitimization: the repeated use of phrases such as 'así era' (16, 358), 'así fue' (219), 'era verdad' (134) reinforces the unmistakably authoritative aspect of Allende's writing. However, such testimonial certainty is kept in check by shifting narrative perspectives which serve to destabilize fixed judgements: Esteban, for example, is generally portrayed as a reactionary and patriarchal figure ironized for his faith in the country's democratic traditions (73) and for his confidence in his own personal integrity and political capabilities (213–14). But the reader's estimation of him is inevitably modified in the light of his first-person accounts. It is difficult, for example, to accept entirely the innocence of Pedro Tercero when his confrontation with Esteban is narrated from Esteban's perspective: 'era mucho más joven que yo y si no podía sorprenderlo estaba jodido' (191). It is his own sense of grievance which informs Esteban's account of his relations with Blanca: 'hablaba menos que su madre y si yo la obligaba a darme un beso de saludo, lo hacía de tan mala gana que me dolía como una bofetada' (171). Similarly it is Clara's insensitivity and ingratitude, for once making her the wrongdoer and him the wronged, that inform his account of her reaction to the lavishly furnished country estate: 'se limitó a encontrarlo todo muy bonito' (172), an assessment that assumes a degree of objectivity since the same phrase is applied to Clara earlier, in Alba's third-person account.

Esteban himself embodies to a certain extent the stylistic diversity of the text. The reader is jolted by Esteban's literary evocations of setting ('al entrar a la zona boscosa, cambió el paisaje y refrescó [...]'), and mood ('yo iba detrás, rumiando mi rabia', 196), extraordinary in a man who claims to have no writing skills (42). The same Esteban who describes his love of women as 'un placer estético, casi espiritual' (173) is also able to deploy the most vulgar language — 'Suelta eso, mocoso de mierda' (198) — which suggests the divide between his private sensibilities and his public violence. The same man who evokes Rosa with poetic sensibility — 'allí estaba Rosa entre blancos pliegues de raso blanco en su blanco ataúd [...]' (39–40) — can also turn his tongue to the curt expression of chauvinistic prejudice: 'su función es la maternidad, el hogar' (70).

In *La casa*, Allende merges two seemingly incompatible narrative modes — the testimonial and the magical realist. Significantly, Alba's testimony needs a miracle to come to fruition (Clara's notebooks 'se salvaron milagrosamente de la pira infame'; 411) and it is not based exclusively on her manuscript sources. Alba's contribution to the text clearly goes beyond editing her grandmother's notebooks: the ten-year-old Clara is unlikely to have recorded her mother Nívea's discomfort in church (14) and it is Alba herself who enters Jaime's mind to uncover his secret desire for her (335). Alba supplements the authoritative version found in the notebooks with her own imaginative reconstructions, mirroring Allende's own procedure. The various references within the text to literature and to literary genres also point to its own literary rather than documentary foundations: Nicolás's sentimental verse is corrected and improved by Amanda (181); Jean de Satigny enthuses over Neruda's sublime poetry (188). There are several instances of life seemingly assuming literary form: Jean, manipulated by Esteban into marriage with Blanca, is left to ponder his story-book situation, 'sin comprender cómo había ido a parar en ese folletín' (205). Jaime's fantasies about Amanda take the form of a fairy tale (226) while Blanca's passionate affair with Pedro Tercero also assumes a literary aura: '[...] la depuró de las verdades prosaicas y pudo convertirla en un amor de novela' (296). The last statement lends itself to a metafictional interpretation since *La casa* itself derives much of its sociopolitical force from its use of magical realist techniques and flamboyant unprosaic language.

It may be argued that the novel gravitates towards literary reference through its conspicuously intertextual relationship with *Cien años de soledad*. Thus several thematic aspects, for example the poisoning of Rosa, and stylistic features such as hyperbole and prolepsis may invoke literary comparisons rather than reference to the real world. Literary technique (and manipulation) emerge explicitly in the reference to Férula's skills as a narrator: 'era una narradora virtuosa, sabía colocar la pausa, medir la entonación, explicar sin gestos [...]' (100). Both Blanca (288) and Alba (405) recycle Marcos's magic stories, Blanca's reinvention of them suggesting Allende's own reinvention of García Márquez's magical realism: Blanca's poor memory means that the stories she tells Alba are virtually new creations. One of these stories is about a prince who 'durmió cien años' while another concerns a wolf which gets lost in the forest and is devoured by a little girl. There may be an implicit reference to García Márquez: is Allende defending herself from charges of plagiarism by pointing to her subversion rather than imitation of the Colombian writer's literary practices? In any event the episode draws attention to narratorial creativity and reinforces the self-conscious side of the text.

The conclusion of the novel is significant here since Alba highlights not so much real historical events as the manner of their documentation by Clara. The last sentence of the text repeats the first part of its opening sentence, both transcriptions of the first words of Clara's first notebook. The final sentence of *La casa* comprises, therefore, a quotation of part of its opening sentence. The ending of the text is introspective and textual rather than external and referential, the text referring back to itself and to its own construction. The closing reference to Clara's 'delicada caligrafía infantil' (411) — recalling the initial allusion to her 'delicada caligrafía' (9) — emphasizes the material process of writing. *La casa* culminates not in serious sociopolitical discourse focusing on events in the world outside the text, but rather in a kind of textual game which encourages the reader to investigate Allende's literary techniques. Her achievement is to have combined testimonial narrative with such self-conscious artistry without diminishing the power and impact of either. *La casa* disturbs the reader with its powerful evocation of sociopolitical events; but it also provides aesthetic pleasure through its self-reflexiveness and linguistic play.

6. Conclusion

The Creative Feminist and the Weaving of the Text

The popular success of *La casa* is not difficult to explain: Cánovas relates it to 'el carácter folletinesco de la anécdota que relata' (*9*, p. 44). The text does, indeed, offer much entertainment irrespective of the readers' level of competence and depends less on their active involvement in unravelling structural and technical difficulties than most other postmodernist works. *Por la patria* (1986) by another Chilean writer, Diamela Eltit, focuses on the political repression of the Pinochet regime and therefore overlaps in thematic coverage with *La casa*; but Eltit, to a far greater extent than Allende, works deliberately and consistently against easy readability. None the less, *La casa*'s greater appeal to the non-competent reader does not imply textual collusion with passive consumption or unreflecting enjoyment: the defamiliarizing effects of Allende's magical realist technnques are certain to challenge any reader. Umberto Eco points out that one can find 'elements of revolution and contestation in works that lend themselves to facile consumption' while other works 'which seem provocative and still enrage the public, do not really contest anything'.[48]

    La casa contests patriarchal assumptions as well as univocal discourse and omniscient narratorial perspective while remaining accessible to the ordinary reader. It is partly because of this accessibility, partly because of its perceived dependence on *Cien años de soledad,* and partly because of the allegedly non-literary

---

[48] Quoted by Matei Calinescu, *Five Faces of Modernity : Modernism, Avante-garde, Decadence, Kitsch, Postmodernism* (Durham, NC: Duke University Press, 1987), p. 285. Eagleton makes a similar point; see note 21, above.

documentation of the final chapters that *La casa* has failed to achieve literary recognition.[49] In addition it is also a difficult text to categorize: thematically it has revolutionary implications, whereas stylistically it is more subdued, rarely challenging the patriarchal order at the level of language. But Allende does contrive significant discursive discontinuity both within and between the narratives of Alba and Esteban; her work offers a balanced combination of traditional and innovative practice. This study has sought to highlight such neglected complexities of *La casa* that even critics generally well disposed towards Allende often fail to acknowledge: its relativization of hegemonic Western rationalist models, its multi-faceted feminist focus and its subtle metafictional aspects. Although the analysis of *La casa*'s relationship with García Márquez's *Cien años* has revealed intimate, and on occasion, even parasitic links — on both thematic and stylistic levels — it has also recognized Allende's creative reconfiguration of the prior male text.

Critical theory appears to have had little impact on Allende, but *La casa*'s connections with certain strands of New Historical writing deserve mention, though *La casa* itself does not qualify as a New Historical text according to the criteria adopted by Seymour Menton.[50] For him the category is reserved for those novels 'whose

---

[49] Few critics seek to defend the novel's conclusion, generally seen as an extraneous appendage deforming the body of the text. One such, however, is Rodrigo Cánovas who claims that 'su testimonio sobre la represión desatada en contra de la izquierda y de las tradiciones democráticas del país resulta eficaz, porque tiene la rapidez, el entusiasmo y la espontaneidad del reportaje periodístico [...]' (*9*, p. 45).

[50] In *Paula* Allende pokes fun at psychoanalysis where she mentions the invention of a machine to measure jealousy and its relative intensity ('el nivel de celotipia') and narrates that 'una sociedad de psiquiatras — no recuerdo si junguianos o lacanianos — nos tomó en serio, fuimos invitados a hacer una demostración [...]' (*1*, 315). Allende may also be capable of mocking the feminist ideal of *écriture féminine*, heavily inscribed by the (female) unconscious and pointing to woman's attunement to sound rather than dry meaning. In *La casa* Clara and Blanca communicate in a language of their own invention 'que suprimía la te al castellano y la remplazaba por ene y la erre por ele, de modo que quedaban hablando igual que el chino de la tintorería' (125–26).

action takes place completely (in some cases, predominantly) in the *past* — arbitrarily defined here as a past not directly experienced by the author' (*32*, p. 16). New Historicism, whose methodology has influenced literary criticism as well as historiography, seeks to challenge official (male) versions of historical writing by diverting attention to the non-canonical, episodic, anecdotal (female) aspects of the historical record which escape or contest the rules, laws, and principles of the dominant codes of their time. Historical writing long excluded the point of view of marginalized groups such as women, the lower classes and non-Europeans. Mysticism is often cited as an example of the repressed other.[51] The organic wholeness of *La casa* emerges when it is seen as a historical text in the broadest sense, recording the marginalized histories of popular custom and mythical belief, articulating the suppressed feminine perspective and staging its conflict with centralized patriarchal power, recuperating the exotic discourse of the magical and the irrational. The perceived structural discontinuity of the text has more to do with critics' persistent demand for uncontaminated discourse — whether literary or historical — than with any actual weaknesses in the text whose ultimate political optimism is constructed on female solidarity and on those female values repudiated by modern society: imagination, intuition, spiritualism, magic. It is these marginalized resources which Allende uses for her own peculiar reconstruction of Chilean history.

The conclusion of the novel has drawn criticism from various quarters. Some critics see no more than arid realism in the final chapters (see *7*, p. 21; *11*, p. 29), while Gabriela Mora objects to the negative ending — Alba bowing to the ineluctable forces of destiny and waiting passively for better times (*20*, p. 55). The conclusion is bleak but the magical elements are never extinguished: the last pages contain the reference to the Mora sisters' superhuman vision which encompasses all past epochs (410); the last line repeats the first line

---

[51] Michel de Certeau, *The Writing of History*, trans. by Tom Conley (New York: Columbia Press, 1988), pp. 249–50. One of the best collection of essays on New Historicism is *New Historicism and Cultural Materialism: A Reader*, ed. by Kiernan Ryan (London: Edward Arnold, 1986).

of the text's strongly magical realist opening and alludes to Barrabás, the dog belonging to Marcos which achieves legendary status. It is not the case therefore that magical realism is banished at the end, merely that it coexists — both in harmony and in conflict, in separation and in fusion — with testimonial discourse. The 'green-woman' archetype is recalled in the final reference to 'vía marítima', that suggests the ebb and flow of female consciousness: the ebb tide of Alba's obsession with destiny gives way to a more positive current, the joyful anticipation of the birth of her daughter, and her seeming indifference to the child's paternity suggests her personal transcendence of patriarchal values. Alba also renounces patriarchal prestige, bestowed by the name of the father, by using her mother's name instead of the aristocratic name — de Satigny — of her putative father (251), following in this respect her uncle, Jaime, who repudiates the Trueba surname (218).[52] The links and chains of destiny point towards a hitherto male-dominated history shackled by impersonal forces and denying even the possibility of human freedom.

The women share a peculiar angelic quality that ranges from the literal (Rosa's physical beauty) to the metaphorical (Alba's self-sacrifice). The angel image can be seen as further undermining of the Freudian idea of woman in need of man to make up her lack since it highlights woman's spiritual, non-sexual aspect. The deepest form of human solidarity portrayed by the text emerges from relations between women: the privacy and uniqueness of the Clara-Blanca

---

[52] In flouting this patriarchal norm, Alba is totally at odds with Esteban Trueba for whom the offspring that matter are those who bear the father's name (70) — a principle of which Esteban García is only too well aware (182). Gilbert and Gubar point out that, for a woman, a proper name is problematic: 'even as it "inscribes" her into the present discourse of society by designating her role as her father's daughter, her patronymic effaces her matrilineage and thus erases her own position in the discourse of the future. Her "proper" name, therefore, is always in a way *im*proper because it is not, in the French sense, *propre*, her own, either to have or to give'. See Sandra M. Gilbert and Susan Gubar, *No Man's Land: The Place of the Woman Writer in the Twentieth Century*, 3 vols (New Haven: Yale University Press, 1988–94), I: *The War of Words*, p. 237.

relationship based on 'la total aceptación mutua [...]' (140) is reflected in their language: 'se comunicaban en un idioma inventado [...]' (125) and excludes Jaime and Nicolás who 'crecían separados del binomio femenino [...]' (126). The pregnant Blanca, certain of her child's gender, communicates with her even before she is born: 'tal como su madre con ella, desarrolló un sistema de comunicación con la criatura que estaba gestando' (239).[53] The subsequent relationship between Clara and Alba is equally intimate: Alba cures Clara of asthma by embracing her (268) and understands perfectly when her grandmother mentions her own imminent death, assuring Alba that it will not separate them but rather bring them closer together (275).

The angel image also represents the otherness of woman and her part-human, part-divine status. Allende's female characters belong to this unstable category which may be seen both as a figure for the forgotten side of a reality that has become stultifyingly familiar, and as the indicator of an alternative to patriarchal political and gender divisions, which it destabilizes through its shifting, uncertain frontiers. Luce Irigaray notes that angels:

> link what has been split by patriarchy — the flesh and the spirit, nature and gods, the carnal and the divine, and are a way of conceptualizing a possible overcoming of the deadly and immobilizing division of the sexes in which women have been allocated body, flesh, nature, earth, carnality while men have been allocated spirit and transcendence.[54]

An important aspect of the female characters (particularly Clara and Alba) is that they are both of this world and not of this

---

[53] The close mother–daughter relationships in *La casa* parallel Allende's intimacy with her own mother: '[...] ella es el amor más largo de mi vida, comenzó el día de mi gestación y ya dura medio siglo, además es el único realmente incondicional, ni los hijos ni los más ardientes enamorados aman así' (*1*, p. 60).

[54] *The Irigaray Reader*, ed. by Margaret Whitford (Oxford: Basil Blackwell, 1991), p. 157.

world (which is literally true of Rosa), both marked by destiny and possessed of the vision to transcend it, both subject to the pleasures and the pains of the body and susceptible to the messages of the spirits, both sensitive to social injustice and committed to the spiritual needs of human beings (reflected in the text's own interweaving of testimonial and imaginative writing). The last pages do not ignore the negative force of destiny — perhaps the most deep-seated of the naturalized patriarchal beliefs and therefore the most difficult to eradicate — but they also point to the possibility of a kind of She-truth through the references to the Mora sisters' capacity to 'ver en el espacio los espíritus de todas las épocas' and to Clara's determination to 'ver las cosas en su dimensión real [...]' (410).[55]

Significantly, the last (implicit) reference to destiny is positive — the miraculous survival of Clara's notebooks following 'la pira infame donde perecieron tantos otros papeles de la familia' (p. 411). Jean Franco argues that the Latin American feminist position, like its French counterpart, is not 'so much one of confronting a dominant patriarchy with a new feminine position but rather one of unsettling the stance that supports gender power/knowledge as masculine' (*34*, pp. 75–76). *La casa* certainly unsettles patriarchal power relations but the text also goes some way towards forging a new feminine position. In their renunciation of vengeance and of the redress to which they are legally entitled, both Esteban and Alba undermine the rule of (masculine) law by following the (female) principles of reconciliation and forgiveness. Esteban's own shift from belligerent authoritarianism towards tolerance of alien personal and political values lends credence to the possibility of a different mode of behaviour which might at first appear to be hopelessly idealistic.

Freud identified weaving — which forms an important activity for Clara (81), Blanca (148) and Alba (267) — as the only contribution of women to the discoveries and inventions in the history of civilization.[56] In *La casa*, male inventions such as the motor car and the aeroplane lead only to death and destruction:

---

[55] Julia Kristeva, *Folle vérité* (Paris: ditions du Seuil, 1979), p.11.
[56] See Naomi Schor, *Breaking the Chain: Women, Theory and French Realist Fiction* (New York: Columbia University Press, 1985), p. 5.

Severo and Nívea are killed in a car accident (120); democracy is finally extinguished by air force bombers which destroy the presidential palace (349). In contrast, the female activity of weaving seeks to meet the most basic human needs and complements Allende's association of woman with nature, but it also has metaphorical significance: weaving suggests textual practice (Alba weaves together the testimony of others) and the tissue of words produced by Clara and Alba is not a finished product but rather an on-going process of interweaving. The strands of death and destiny remain but the binding is formed from the female logic of reconciliation and openness to a different future — which cannot be dismissed as an idealized female vision with scant chance of ever materializing. The female mode of doing and writing has already refined the coarse texture of Esteban's patriarchal character and stands out finally as the text's last word.

Esteban's discourse of authority and power, unrestrained at the outset, appears subdued and tempered by female values at the conclusion. The text generally highlights positive female values in opposition to their male patriarchal counterparts, often suggesting a rigid binary divide between them.[57] It is well to remember, however, that Clara's abstraction is frequently ironized and the (male) rigour of the punishment she inflicts on Esteban is not reduced, despite his (female) devotion and desire for reconciliation. Though the text owes, in different ways, its existence to three women, Clara, Alba, and Tránsito Soto, it is Esteban's (male) initiative, now harnessed to positive objectives, which provides the initial impetus for its production. What may at first appear to be a sharp contrast between good (generally represented by the female characters) and evil (generally represented by the male) loses its clarity in retrospect. *La casa* is a feminist (and female) work which avoids facile simplifications: it is, above all, a heterogeneous and dialogical text

---

[57] Allende is certainly guilty of crude essentialism in her presentation of character for which she often uses the same verbal formulae: Nicolás discovers the urge to fly that 'siempre estuvo presente en los hombres de su estirpe' (20); peasant women lower their heads 'por la costumbre ancestral de todas las mujeres de su estirpe de bajar la cabeza ante el macho' (61–62).

which interweaves the tragic and the comic, the historical and the fictional, the commonplace and the fantastic, resisting compliance with any form of masculine orthodoxy and undermining the validity of those binary oppositions upon which the order of patriarchal logic is founded.

Bibliographical Note

A.   ISABEL ALLENDE: WRITINGS AND INTERVIEWS

1. *Paula* (1994), 6th edn (Barcelona: Plaza & Janés, 1995). An often harrowing account of her daughter's death which also offers insights into Allende's psychology and literary priorities.
2. 'Writing as an Act of Hope', *in Paths of Resistance: the Art and Craft of the Political Novel: Isabel Allende, Charles McCarry, Marge Piercy, Robert Stone, Gore Vidal*, ed. by William Zinsser (Boston: Houghton Mifflin, 1989), pp. 39–63. A general discussion touching on magical realism, patriarchy, and the possibility of a different future based on female values.
3. 'La magia de las palabras', *Revista Iberoamericana*, 51 (1985), 447–52. A lyrical tribute to the sensuous potentialities of the Spanish language accompanied by an outline of the gestation, publication, and impact of *La casa*.
4. Ignacio Carrión, 'Isabel Allende: entrevista', *El País*, 28 November 1993, pp. 48–59. The broad range of issues covered include her psychological conditioning by the powerful patriarchs in her family, the impact of her daughter's death, and her views on literature.
5. Magdalena García Pinto, 'Entrevista con Isabel Allende en Nueva York, abril 1985', *Historias íntimas: conversaciones con diez escritoras latinoamericanas* (Hanover, NH: Ediciones del Norte, 1988), pp. 3–26. An early interview providing some useful information on her attitude to men — both fictional (Esteban Trueba) and real (García Márquez).
6. John Rodden, '"The Responsibility to Tell You": an Interview with Isabel Allende', *Kenyon Review*, 13 (1991), 113–23. Focuses on Allende's sociopolitical commitment.

B. CRITICAL STUDIES ON ISABEL ALLENDE

7. Robert Antoni, 'Parody or Piracy: The Relationship of *The House of the Spirits* to *One Hundred Years of Solitude* ', *Latin American Literary Review*, 16 (1988), 16–28. Reviews the most obvious, mainly stylistic,

similarities, arguing that Allende unconsciously parodies García Márquez in the first part of *La casa*.

8. Gloria Bautista Gutiérrez, *Realismo mágico, cosmos latinoamericano: teoría y práctica* (Bogotá: América Latina, 1991), pp. 44–125. A painstaking comparison of *Cien años* and *La casa*, investigating their treatment of such themes as time, solitude, love, and death.

9. Rodrigo Cánovas, 'Los espíritus literarios y políticos de Isabel Allende', in *13*, pp. 37–47. A useful commentary on the first chapter of *La casa* leads to a thought-provoking consideration of the García Márquez-Allende relationship in terms of 'un humilde servidor y una alegre antropófaga'.

10. Susan de Carvalho, 'The Male Narrative Perspective in the Fiction of Isabel Allende', *Journal of Hispanic Research*, 2 (1993–94), 269–78. A lucid discussion of the evolution of the masculine perspective (in both *La casa* and *El plan infinito*) and the emergence of the 'post-masculine' male.

11. Laurie Clancy, 'Isabel Allende's Dialogue with García Márquez: A Study in Literary Debt', *Antípodas*, 6–7 (1994–95), 29–43. Points to what Clancy sees as Allende's often parasitic dependence on García Márquez but regards her faith in the social power of literature as an important distinguishing feature.

12. Marcelo Coddou, *Para leer a Isabel Allende: introducción a 'La casa de los espíritus'* (Concepción, Chile: LAR, 1988). The leading Allende critic offers illuminating comments on the major aspects of Allende's work, refuting the view that it is cyclical and pessimistic. His exaggerated classification of her realism as 'suprareferencialidad' is a slight aberration in an otherwise balanced and informative study.

13. *Critical Approaches to Isabel Allende's Novels*, ed. by Sonia Riquelme Rojas and Edna Aguirre Rehbein, American University Studies, 22, Latin American Literature, 14 (New York: Peter Lang, 1991). The useful essays on *La casa* cover Allende's treatment of prostitution, the dissolution of the happy family, and the bonds uniting the female characters. See *9* above for Cánovas's contribution.

14. Susan Frenk, 'The Wandering Text: Situating the Narratives of Isabel Allende' in *Latin American Women's Writing: Feminist Readings in Theory and Crisis*, ed. by Anny Brooksbank Jones and Catherine Davies, Oxford Hispanic Studies (Oxford: Clarendon Press, 1996), pp. 66–84. Argues cogently that Allende subverts the social naturalization of sex-gender relations, noting in particular the mother–daughter bond as unassimilable to the patriarchal norm.

15. Patricia Hart, *Narrative Magic in the Fiction of Isabel Allende* (London: Associated University Presses, 1989). Coins a new term, 'magical feminism', to denote magical realism in a 'femino-centric' work, but goes on to argue that magic is consistently undercut by reality.

16. Teresa Huerta, 'La ambivalencia de la violencia y el horror en *La casa de los espíritus* de Isabel Allende', *Chasqui,* 19 (1990), 56–63. Locates *La casa* within a novelistic tradition dedicated to the investigation of institutionalized injustice.

17. Linda Gould Levine, 'Isabel Allende', in *Spanish American Women Writers: A Bio-bibliographical Guide*, ed. by Diane E. Marting (Westport, CT: Greenwood, 1990), pp. 20–30. Provides a useful overview in three sections: biography, major themes, and survey of criticism.

18. *Los libros tienen sus propios espíritus*, ed. by Marcelo Coddou (Xalapa: Universidad de Veracruz, 1986). An important collection of essays, particularly strong on feminism and narrative technique.

19. Z. Nelly Martínez, 'The Politics of the Woman Artist in Isabel Allende's *The House of the Spirits*', in *Writing the Woman Artist: Essays on Poetics, Politics and Portraiture*, ed. by Suzanne W. Jones (Philadelphia: University of Pennsylvania Press, 1991), pp. 287–306. A penetrating account of Allende's indictment of patriarchy focusing, on the subversive qualities of the female characters who are seen as latter-day witches.

20. Gabriela Mora, 'Las novelas de Isabel Allende y el papel de la mujer como ciudadana', *Ideologies and Literature*, 2 (1987), 53–61. A trenchant though largely unconvincing criticism of *La casa*, which focuses on such aspects as Esteban's death (seen as inappropriately benign), on Alba's passivity, and on the fatalistic mood of the conclusion, while largely ignoring the positive presentation of alternative, female values.

21. *La narrativa de Isabel Allende: claves de una marginalidad*, ed. by Adriana Castillo de Berchenko, Marges, 6 (Perpignan: CRILAUP, Université de Perpignan, 1990). A useful volume containing a bibliography of Allende criticism, interviews, and a variety of essays on *La casa.*

22. Donald L. Shaw, *The Post-Boom in Spanish American Fiction*, SUNY Series in Latin American and Iberian Thought and Culture (Albany, NY: State University of New York Press, 1998), pp. 53–72. A penetrating analysis of Allende's work, highlighting her Post-Boom ambivalence towards reality which she knows to be inexpressible yet strives to grasp none the less. Emphasizes her strong presentation of women while noting her formulation of social problems in terms of naive emotional idealism.

23. Philip Swanson, 'Tyrants and Trash: Sex, Class and Culture in *La casa de los espíritus*', *Bulletin of Hispanic Studies*, 71 (1994), 217–37. A wide-ranging critique, emphasizing the political commitment and emotional power of the text whose apparent freedom from the influence of feminist theory does little to diminish the force of its message.

24. Nicasio Urbina, '*La casa de los espíritus* de Isabel Allende y *Cien años de soledad* de Gabriel García Márquez: un modelo retórico común', *Escritura*, 15.29 (1990), 215–28. A detailed analysis of the thematic and stylistic links between *Cien años* and *La casa*, claiming with some justification to have established a direct line of influence.

C. BACKGROUND STUDIES

(i) Critical

25. Debra A. Castillo, *Talking Back: Toward a Latin American Feminist Literary Criticism* (Ithaca: Cornell University Press, 1992). A firm grasp of feminist theory is brought to bear on the elucidation of the Latin American 'difference'. Offers useful background reading; negative comments on Allende's alleged 'institutionalization' of female subservience are reminiscent of Gabriela Mora's approach.
26. Amaryll Beatrice Chanady, *Magical Realism and the Fantastic: Resolved Versus Unresolved Antinomies* (New York: Garland, 1985). Focuses on 'antinomy' (the simultaneous presence of two conflicting codes in the text), and draws a helpful distinction between the magical realist and the fantastic modes.
27. Santiago Colás, *Postmodernity in Latin America* : *The Argentine Paradigm* (Durham, NC: Duke University Press, 1994). Competent treatment of the Latin American inflections of postmodernism, complemented by skilful handling of major commentators such as Linda Hutcheon and Fredric Jameson.
28. Aníbal González, *Journalism and the Development of Spanish American Narrative*, Cambridge Studies in Latin American and Iberian Literature (Cambridge: Cambridge University Press, 1993). Traces the peculiar relationship between narrative fiction and journalism in Latin America and considers the moral dilemmas which documentary narratives pose for the reader.
29. Amy Katz Kaminsky, *Reading the Body Politic: Feminist Criticism and Latin American Women Writers* (Minneapolis: University of Minnesota Press, 1993). A readable account, particularly helpful on testimonial writing and its precarious position at the boundaries of fiction and non-fiction.
30. Jo Labanyi, *Myth and History in the Contemporary Spanish Novel* (Cambridge: Cambridge University Press, 1989). The introductory chapter, on the historical uses of myth, presents an excellent overview, investigating the various renewals of myth (taken in the Romantic sense

of original state of innocence prior to civilization) and considering the specific Latin American context.

31. *Magical Realism: Theory, History, Community*, ed. by Lois Parkinson Zamora and Wendy B. Faris (Durham, NC: Duke University Press, 1995). An important collection offering both early general essays such as Alejo Carpentier's 'On the Marvelous Real in America' (1949) and recent comparative work, for example, P. Gabrielle Foreman's investigation of history and the 'magically real' in Toni Morrison and Allende.

32. Seymour Menton, *Latin America's New Historical Novel* (Austin: University of Texas Press, 1993). An excellent opening chapter on definitions and origins is somewhat marred by the adoption of Enrique Anderson Imbert's restriction of the category 'historical novel' to works whose action occurs in a period previous to the author's. *La casa* is therefore excluded although it displays many of the New Historical characteristics outlined by Menton.

33. Seymour Menton, *Magical Realism Rediscovered, 1918–1981* (London: Associated University Presses, 1983). A fascinating synopsis of the uses of the term both in the arts and in literature.

34. *On Edge: The Crisis of Contemporary Latin American Culture*, ed. by George Yúdice, Jean Franco, and Juan Flores, Cultural Politics, 4 (Minneapolis: University of Minnesota Press, 1992). An important contribution to the debate on the complex configurations of Latin American culture, with Franco's discussion of testimonial writing and Yúdice's of postmodernity in Latin America providing valuable background information for contextualizing Allende's work.

35. Emir Rodríguez Monegal, 'Carnaval/Antropofagia/Parodia', *Revista Iberoamericana*, 45 (1979), 401–12. A seminal study of the reception of Bakhtinian thought in the Latin American cultural sphere.

36. Elzbieta Sklodowska, *Testimonio hispanoamericano: historia, teoría, poética* (New York: Peter Lang, 1992). Traces the background of Latin America's supposedly native genre and analyses its problematical truth claims as well as its links with postmodernism.

37. Gianni Vattimo, *The Transparent Society*, trans. by David Webb (Cambridge: Polity Press, 1992). Offers fresh insights into the nature and function of myth.

38. Raymond Leslie Williams, *The Postmodern Novel in Latin America: Politics, Culture and the Crisis of Truth* (London: Macmillan, 1995). The opening chapter offers an outline of the major issues, noting the influence on Latin American writing of European theorists, such as Gadamer and Ricouer. The precise relationship between the 'Postmodern' and the 'Post-Boom' remains unclarified since the latter term is not used.

(ii) Historical

39. Patricia Chuchryk, 'From Dictatorship to Democracy: The Women's Movement in Chile', in *The Women's Movement in Latin America: Participation and Democracy*, ed. by Jane S. Jacquette (Boulder, CO: Westview, 1994), pp. 65–107. An enlightening account which points to the established hold of male authoritarianism on Chilean family life prior to its eruption on the national political stage in 1973.

40. Paul Drake, 'Chile, 1930–58', and Alan Angell, 'Chile since 1958' in *The Cambridge History of Latin America*, ed. by Leslie Bethell (Cambridge: Cambridge University Press, 1984–), VIII (1991): *Latin America since 1930: Spanish South America*, pp. 269–310; pp. 311–82. Both writers offer detailed and balanced surveys elucidating the complexities of the periods covered.

41. Eduardo Galeano, *Las venas abiertas de América Latina*, 65th edn (Mexico City: Siglo XXI, 1993). A trenchant analysis highlighting foreign, particularly U.S., responsibility for the injustices besetting the region.

42. Asunción Lavrin, *Women, Feminism, and Social Change in Argentina, Chile and Uruguay, 1890–1940*, Engendering Latin America, 3 (Lincoln: University of Nebraska Press, 1995). A meticulously-documented and well-indexed account of the evolution of feminism which illuminates some of the issues raised in *La casa*.

43. Gerda Lerner, *Women and History* (New York: Oxford University Press, 1986), I: *The Creation of Patriarchy*. Provides a lucid and convincing explanation of the rise and self-perpetuating resilience of the patriarchal system and of women's position within it.

44. Brian Loveman, *Chile: the Legacy of Hispanic Capitalism*, 2nd edn (New York: Oxford University Press, 1988). A consistently analytical and highly readable account, particularly perceptive on the reasons for Salvador Allende's downfall.

45. Edwin Williamson, *The Penguin History of Latin America* (Harmondsworth: Penguin, 1992). The excellent chapter on Chile, with separate sections on the Allende and Pinochet eras, offers relevant and concise background reading.

CRITICAL GUIDES TO SPANISH TEXTS

Edited by
Alan Deyermond and Stephen Hart

CRITICAL GUIDES TO SPANISH TEXTS

Edited by
Alan Deyermond and Stephen Hart